LAWS AND EXPLANATION
IN HISTORY

LAWS AND EXPLANATION IN HISTORY

BY

WILLIAM DRAY

Assistant Professor of Philosophy
The University of Toronto

OXFORD UNIVERSITY PRESS

Oxford University Press, Amen House, London E.C.4

GLASGOW NEW YORK TORONTO MELBOURNE WELLINGTON
BOMBAY CALCUTTA MADRAS KARACHI LAHORE DACCA
CAPE TOWN SALISBURY NAIROBI IBADAN ACCRA
KUALA LUMPUR HONG KONG

First published 1957 in the
OXFORD CLASSICAL & PHILOSOPHICAL MONOGRAPHS
and reprinted lithographically in 1960
Third impression reprinted lithographically
at the University Press, Oxford
1964

PREFACE

IN this book I offer a discussion of the logical structure of explanation as it is given in ordinary historical writing. As the title suggests, I attempt to deal only with a certain aspect of this problem: the extent to which the giving of explanation in history requires knowledge of laws. Certain contributions to a general theory of explanation do emerge at various stages of the argument, but my main purpose is to show why I think a very prevalent view of the relation between laws and explanation unacceptable. The immediate argument arises out of a consideration of the views expressed on this subject by a number of contemporary philosophers in Britain and America, and especially by Mr. P. L. Gardiner in *The Nature of Historical Explanation*, which was published in the Oxford Classical and Philosophical Monographs Series a few years ago.

It is a pleasure to be able to acknowledge the very great debt I owe to my teacher in philosophy, Mr. W. H. Walsh. Without his guidance, and the stimulation of his own work in philosophy of history, this book would have been much worse than it is. Without his encouragement, it would not have existed at all. My thanks are also due to the many friends, especially Professor D. G. Brown and the Rev. D. D. Evans, who took time to dispute with me on a number of points; to Professor G. Ryle and Professor H. H. Price, who gave me valuable criticisms of the whole work in typescript; and to my wife, who added understanding and forbearance to active help of many kinds. I am grateful, too, to the Humanities Research Council of Canada for assistance in the form of a research grant, and to the Warden and Fellows of Nuffield College, Oxford, for making me a member of their society during the final stage of the work.

The book is a shortened version of the greater part of a thesis which was submitted for the D.Phil. degree at Oxford University in Michaelmas Term, 1955.

W. D.

Oxford
May, 1957

CONTENTS

I

THE COVERING LAW MODEL

1. *Statement of the Model*

IN recent years philosophers of history have had to reckon with a general theory of explanation which, in spite of its prestige among logicians, has often appeared to fit rather awkwardly the explanations historians actually give. To put it in a summary way, what the theory maintains is that explanation is achieved, and only achieved, *by subsuming what is to be explained under a general law.* Such an account of the basic structure of all explanation is sometimes referred to as 'the regularity analysis'; but because it makes use of the notion of bringing a case under a law, i.e. 'covering' it with a law, I shall often speak of it hereafter as 'the covering law model'.[1] In the chapters to follow I shall argue that whether or not it has a use in other fields, it is a dangerous model for the philosophy of history. For it commonly leads its advocates into talking about explanation in history in ways which are either radically incorrect or misleading in important respects.

Covering law theory is to be found variously formulated. Indeed, one of the difficulties in the way of any attempt to assess its adequacy is that of discovering exactly what its exponents intend to assert when they move beyond such summary characterizations as the one given above. Let me begin, therefore, by drawing attention to some of the things covering law theorists have actually written.

Professor K. R. Popper, who claims to be the author of the model, having put it forward as a general theory of explanation in 1935 in *Logik der Forschung,* and again ten years later in *The Open Society and Its Enemies* with particular reference

---

[1] P. L. Gardiner calls it "the regularity interpretation" in *The Nature of Historical Explanation,* Oxford, 1952, p. 65. See also pp. 70, 82. For a hint of 'covering law' terminology see R. B. Braithwaite's *Scientific Explanation,* Cambridge, 1953, p. 1.

to history, puts his central doctrine thus: "To give a *causal explanation* of a certain event means to derive deductively a statement (it will be called a *prognosis*) which describes that event, using as premises of the deduction some *universal laws* together with certain singular or specific sentences which we may call *initial conditions*." He continues: "The initial conditions (or more precisely, the situation described by them) are usually spoken of as the *cause* of the event in question, and the prognosis (or rather, the event described by the prognosis) as the effect. . . ."[1]

In *The Open Society* Popper goes on to draw some consequences from this theory. One important consequence is the discovery of a close logical connexion between explanation, prediction, and confirmation. According to Popper, "the use of a theory for the purpose of *predicting* some specific event is just another aspect of its use for the purpose of *explaining* such an event", and the notions of *confirming* or *testing* are related in a similar way. In terms of this logical pattern it is possible to distinguish three sorts of sciences, all using the covering law model, but for different purposes and in different ways. The 'pure generalizing sciences' (e.g. physics, biology, sociology) use it to test, and hence to establish 'universal laws or hypotheses', referring to specific events only in order to do this. The 'applied generalizing sciences' (e.g. engineering) are interested in the prognosis, i.e. a prediction of a specific event, using the universal laws as means only, and taking their truth for granted. The 'historical sciences', on the other hand, are "interested in explaining a specific or particular event", rather than predicting or testing. Historians are not concerned to formulate or establish laws; what they do is 'assume' them. Popper believes that this analysis shows both why history has been said to be a study of the particular, and why this fact nevertheless cannot be cited as a reason for denying that the historian, like the natural scientist, uses general laws.

Popper's account of explanation would, I think, generally be spoken of as 'positivist'. It appears in various guises in the

[1] Quoted in *The Open Society*, London, 1952, vol. ii, p. 262.

writings of analytic philosophers influenced by the logical positivist movement of the twenties and thirties; and it is anticipated in the work of the nineteenth-century positivists Comte and Mill. Its advocacy is part of a reforming approach to the social studies, a deliberate attempt to make history more 'scientific'—in the present instance by insisting on rigorous logical standards for what may count as explanation. Its general intellectual groove, of course, can be traced back farther —for instance to the classical discussion of causality by Hume. Indeed, many modern exponents of the model explicitly acknowledge their indebtedness to Hume. Popper states his relation to Hume thus:

. . . [Hume] pointed out (as against the Cartesian view) that we cannot know anything about a necessary connection between an event A and another event B. . . . Our theory fully recognizes this Humean criticism. But it differs from Hume (1) in that it explicitly formulates the *universal hypothesis* that events of the kind A are always and everywhere followed by events of the kind B; (2) that it asserts the truth of the statement that A is the cause of B, provided that the universal hypothesis is true. Hume, in other words, only looked at the events A and B themselves; and he could not find any trace of a causal link or a necessary connection between these two. But we add a third thing, a universal law; and with respect to this law, we may speak of a causal link, or even of a necessary connection.[1]

Popper's point is taken up and developed by Professor C. G. Hempel in a lucid and influential article entitled, 'The Function of General Laws in History'.[2] Hempel generalizes the covering law model beyond the strictly causal form, and endeavours to show in more detail how it can be successfully applied to historical cases. His formulation of the ideal, which is more rigorous than Popper's, reads thus:

The explanation of the occurrence of an event of some specific kind E at a certain place and time consists, as it is usually expressed, in indicating the causes or determining factors of E. Now the assertion that a set of events—say, of the kinds $C_1, C_2, \ldots, C_n$—have caused the event to be explained amounts to the statement that, according to certain general

---

[1] Op. cit., p. 343.
[2] Reprinted in *Readings in Philosophical Analysis*, ed. H. Feigl and W. Sellars, New York, 1949, pp. 459–71.

laws, a set of events of the kinds mentioned is regularly accompanied by an event of kind E. Thus, the scientific explanation of the event in question consists of

(1) a set of statements asserting the occurrence of certain events $C_1, \ldots,$ C_n at certain times and places,
(2) a set of universal hypotheses, such that
   (a) the statements of both groups are reasonably well confirmed by empirical evidence,
   (b) from the two groups of statements the sentence asserting the occurrence of event E can be logically deduced.

In a physical explanation, group (1) would describe the initial and boundary conditions for the occurrence of the final event; generally, we shall say that group (1) states the *determining conditions* for the event to be explained, while group (2) contains the general laws on which the explanation is based; they imply the statement that whenever events of the kind described in the first group occur, an event of the kind to be explained will take place.[1]

It will be noticed that the model outlined is said to give the logical structure of 'scientific' explanation, particularly that found in the most developed of the natural sciences: physics. But, as I have already suggested, it is generally part of the purpose of advocates of the model to vindicate the 'scientific' character of history—or, perhaps more accurately, to forestall the conclusion that history may operate successfully with procedures and criteria of its own. Hempel's scientism appears in uncompromising form in the dichotomy which he draws between *scientific* and *pseudo* explanation. Any alleged explanation must be either one or the other. Thus, when he goes on to consider historical cases, the only peculiarities he finds reduce to matters of precision or articulation.

Hempel gives two reasons for the common failure to realize that general laws "have a theoretical function" in explanations given in history as well as in science. He points out, first, that the laws in question are not only taken as known and established, i.e. used rather than discovered, but as so well known that in most cases they are not mentioned at all. They are to be regarded as only *implicit* in the proffered explanation. This is

[1] pp. 459-60.

particularly the case, he believes, with generalizations about human nature. In *The Open Society* Popper makes a similar, although not identical, suggestion when he writes: "Although an event is the cause of another event, which is its effect, only relative to some universal law, in history the latter are often so trivial that as a rule we take them for granted instead of making conscious use of them." And he adds the following illustration:

If we explain, for example, the first division of Poland in 1772 by pointing out that it could not possibly resist the combined power of Russia, Prussia and Austria, then we are tacitly using some trivial universal law such as: 'If of two armies which are about equally well armed and led, one has a tremendous superiority in men, then the other never wins.' . . . Such a law might be described as a law of the sociology of military power; but it is too trivial ever to raise a serious problem for the students of sociology, or to arouse their attention. Or if we explain Caesar's decision to cross the Rubicon by his ambition and energy, say, then we are using some very trivial psychological generalizations which would hardly ever arouse the attention of a psychologist.[1]

The second reason given by Hempel for the widespread failure to recognize the historian's use of general laws is that it is usually very difficult to formulate the laws in question "with sufficient precision and at the same time in such a way that they are in agreement with all the relevant empirical evidence available". For what the historian offers under these conditions Hempel coins the term, 'explanation sketch'. The sketch, he says, "consists of a more or less vague indication of the laws and initial conditions considered as relevant, and it needs 'filling out' in order to turn into a full-fledged explanation. This filling out requires further empirical research, for which the sketch suggests the direction." The important point is that although the laws may only be vaguely suggested, they could be stated more precisely if the historian did his job more thoroughly. The logical theory of the covering law consequently stands unassailed; the difference between the historian's sketch and an ideal 'scientific' explanation is in the former's lack of precision, not in its logical form.

[1] Op. cit., pp. 264-5.

Hempel's analysis is designed to convince us that in so far as explanation is given in history, it is given, in spite of appearances to the contrary, on the covering law model. On one question, however, he professes himself "entirely neutral": whether explanation in history is a special kind, achieved, for example, by means of "specifically historical laws". It is to this question that another covering law theorist, Professor M. G. White, turns in a carefully argued article entitled 'Historical Explanation'.[1] Having registered his approval of Hempel's essential thesis, White asks: 'What, then, is the nature of specifically *historical* explanation?' And he goes on to consider various possibilities in the light of covering law theory.

One possibility which suggests itself is that the distinguishing mark of an historical explanation is reference to the past, i.e. "a historical explanation explains facts at one time by reference to facts prevailing at an earlier time". Thus one might distinguish between two kinds of laws which can perform the covering function: those which contain some reference to a lapse of time, and those which do not. But White argues that to define historical explanation in terms of the use of temporal laws only is to adopt too broad a criterion. For there are laws which we now rightly regard as belonging to one or other of the natural sciences which would have to be called historical if this test were accepted; and "we do not want our analysis to result in the statement that one explanation is both mechanical and historical".

In the hope of finding a more satisfactory criterion of 'historical' explanation by contrast with, for example, 'mechanical' or 'physical' or 'biological', White asks on what principle we ordinarily decide that explanations are of a certain kind, i.e. belong to a certain science. The distinction, he maintains, is made on the basis of the essential employment of technical terms native to the science concerned. Thus a chemical explanation is identified by the occurrence of 'element' words like 'hydrogen', and no explanation in which such terms do not occur essentially can be counted as specifically chemical. It is

[1] *Mind*, 1943, pp. 212-29.

necessary to say 'essentially' in order to rule out purely analytic truths accidentally employing technical terms, and also to allow for the fact that most sciences, because they are related to each other in a logical hierarchy, presuppose other sciences, and thus terms of the presupposed sciences occur (although 'unessentially') in the statements of the presupposing sciences. Physics, for instance, is presupposed by most other sciences; logic is presupposed by all, while itself presupposing none. The existence of historical explanations, therefore, depends on the existence of specifically historical terms; and any explanation in which such terms occur essentially will properly be regarded as an historical explanation.

But whereas the first criterion considered had the disadvantage of allowing too many explanations to be called 'historical', White doubts that *any* could qualify on the present one. For history is the polar opposite of logic in that it presupposes *all* the other sciences, and has *no* special technical terms of its own; they are all borrowed. Terms which may at first appear to be specifically historical ones, e.g. 'revolution', usually turn out to belong to the science of sociology. Like most positivists, and as Popper had already contended, White concludes that history differs from sociology only in applying rather than discovering the laws of social phenomena. The answer to the question: 'What is the nature of historical explanation?' is therefore: 'There are no such explanations.' The explanations which historians give, in so far as they are reputable, must be 'scientific' (and generally sociological) ones.

2. *Reception by Philosophers and Historians*

The statement of the covering law theory and its implications which has been given above is drawn from the writings of three contemporary philosophers who have been in the forefront of recent controversy in the philosophy of history. But, as I have already suggested, their view of the nature of explanation is far from being an isolated one, and something like it can, in fact, be found in the work of many American and British philosophers and social theorists, with and without reference to the authors already mentioned. The theory might, indeed, be said to have achieved, in many quarters, the status of accepted doctrine.

Thus, according to Professor C. J. Ducasse, "explanation essentially consists in the offering of a hypothesis of fact, standing to the fact to be explained as a case of antecedent to case of consequent of some already known law of connection...".[1] According to Professor F. Kaufmann, "it is elliptical to speak of a cause of a given event without referring explicitly to the law in terms of which it is a cause of the event".[2] According to Professor R. B. Braithwaite, "to ask for the cause of an event is always to ask for a general law which applies to the particular event".[3] Similar statements can be found in the work of many other writers, to some of whom reference will later be made. The unassailability of the model appears to have reached the point where an extreme version of it can be introduced apologetically into a symposium of the Aristotelian Society as "a rather obvious point to be made about causal explanation in general".[4]

Opposition to covering law theory, or at any rate to the *kind* of thinking about history which it represents, has come mainly from philosophers who could be called 'idealist'. The most uncompromising opponents simply declare 'the autonomy of history', claiming that the historian has no dealings whatever with general laws, and yet explains his subject-matter quite satisfactorily in his own way. If we ask for more details about the way explanations should proceed in history, we are likely to receive an answer drawn from a view of the peculiar nature of the historian's subject-matter. Thus Professor M. Oakeshott, in *Experience and Its Modes*, having emphasized the inexhaustible particularity, the uniqueness, of historical events, represents historical explanation as simply

[1] 'Explanation, Mechanism and Teleology', reprinted in Feigl and Sellars, *Readings in Philosophical Analysis*, p. 540.
[2] *The Methodology of the Social Sciences*, New York, 1944, p. 93.
[3] Op. cit., p. 2.
[4] R. S. Peters, 'Motives and Causes', *Proceedings of the Aristotelian Society, Supp. Vol.*, 1952, p. 141.

"a full account of change"—the most complete and detailed description of what is to be explained that the historian is capable of giving. For Oakeshott, not only has the notion of 'law' no place in historical explanation, but the category of 'cause' itself is "replaced by the exhibition of a world of events intrinsically related to one another in which no *lacuna* is tolerated".[1]

In *The Idea of History* R. G. Collingwood dispenses with the notion of 'law' in the light of a different aspect of the historian's subject-matter: the fact that it is past human action, which has a 'thought-side'. In history "the object to be discovered is not the mere event but the thought expressed in it. To discover that thought is already to understand it."[2] It is Collingwood's contention that once the thought-side of the action is revealed, bringing the action under law can add nothing to our understanding of it. For "the value of generalization in natural science depends on the fact that the data of physical science are given by perception, and perceiving is not understanding". In the case of human actions, where direct understanding is possible, we therefore demand more than that intelligibility which comes from recognizing "the relations between general types".[3] Like Oakeshott, Collingwood claims that explanation on the covering law model, if it were given in history, would be in one way or another inappropriate or out of place.

But few idealist writers—even the two unquestionably vigorous ones mentioned—have succeeded in putting their counter-argument in a form comparable in clarity and precision with that of their opponents, and their position has in recent years tended to go by default. There have, nevertheless, been some attempts to do justice to both sides, giving qualified acceptance to covering law theory, but seeking to modify it in the light of idealist doctrines. Thus Professor M. Mandelbaum, in *The Problem of Historical Knowledge*, although appearing to accept something like the covering law analysis of explanation, and a similar analysis of the concepts of 'relevance' and 'importance', at one crucial point insists

[1] Cambridge, 1953, p. 143.   [2] Oxford, 1946, p. 214.   [3] Op. cit., pp. 222-3.

that the historian's task is to exhibit events in their "actual
determining relationships". And he denies that such "full
causal explanation" is reducible without remainder to subsumption under covering law.[1]

In *An Introduction to Philosophy of History* Mr. W. H.
Walsh also argues for a compromise.[2] Against Collingwood's
apparent claim that human actions are understood "in a single
act of intuitive insight", Walsh points out that in order to
grasp and understand the thought of historical agents we have
to interpret historical evidence, "and this process of interpretation is one in which we make at least implicit reference
to general truths". Unlike Collingwood and Oakeshott, Walsh
recognizes a wide sphere of application for the covering law
model in history; yet he makes it clear that he regards the
laws implicit in the explanation of most individual actions in
history as peculiar in important ways. What the historian
brings to his study of the past, Walsh maintains, is a basic, non-
technical knowledge of human nature—a kind of 'common
sense'—which it is very difficult to regard as arrived at by any
ordinary process of induction. For this would do "less than
justice to the subtlety and depth of insight into the possibilities of human nature shown by the great historians".[3]

The reception of the model by historians themselves has
also been divided. A few, like Professor R. M. Crawford, have
hailed it with enthusiasm—less as a faithful reflection of the
way historical inquiry proceeds than as an instrument of
emancipation and progress: one more step in a century-long
march "in the direction of making historical studies more
scientific". In an article entitled 'History as a Science',[4]
having confessed that theoretical problems of his subject
drove him to "turn for help to the philosophers", Crawford
denies that we can ever speak of 'actual determining relationships' without assuming that the events concerned represent instances of regular relationships formulable as laws—

---

[1] New York, 1938, p. 14.   [2] London, 1951, chap. iii.
[3] I shall show (in Chaps. II and V) that both Mandelbaum's and Walsh's
views are suggestive of ways in which covering law theory requires modification.
[4] *Historical Studies, Australia and New Zealand*, 1947, pp. 153-4.

although the prudence of an historian leads him to add that such a contention does not require the exact repetition of events. Crawford has no hesitation in using the model to assess the adequacy of explanations which historians have actually given, and he clearly expects a marked improvement in historical writing to result from a more general determination among historians to make the covering laws assumed by their explanations explicit.

The persuasive appeal of the model to reformers may also be seen in a remarkable bulletin published by the American Social Science Research Council, entitled *Theory and Practice in Historical Studies*.[1] This pamphlet outlines the conclusions reached by a committee of historians who had the temerity to call upon a philosopher, Professor S. Hook, for light on their subject. The essentials of covering law doctrine are plainly expounded in Hook's declaration: "An event or process is explained if it can be shown that it follows from a set of relevant antecedent events regarded as determining conditions.... [It] always involves the assumption of some general laws or statistical generalizations relating classes of phenomena, to one of which the event or process belongs."[2] The only peculiarities of explanation in history are said to be (1) that its subject-matter is confined to "human activity in social contexts", (2) that the laws involved are comparatively vague, and (3) that the historian's research techniques are autonomous, although the logic of evidence is not. Hook's account was incorporated into a final 'statement of faith' by his historical colleagues.

As a rule, however, historians tend to resist the model as in some way irrelevant to what they are trying to do. Unfortunately, they do not always make it clear why they think this is so. Some register their protest in metaphorical rather than argumentative terms. Thus Butterfield has deplored the attempt to write history on "geometrical patterns with clean

---

[1] *Bulletin No. 54*, New York, 1946.
[2] Op. cit., p. 127. Hook is here outlining just one of two possible views, but we are left in little doubt that it is this one he accepts.

white spaces (where there ought to be a rich, thick under-growth) between the lines".[1] And Trevelyan has insisted that Clio is a Muse, without showing precisely what is wrong with a 'scientific' approach.[2] Other historians, unable to deny that the model has a certain *a priori* plausibility, concede the logical point, and make its inapplicability to history only a matter of difficulty in practice. And, of course, there are always some who find it attractive to retreat to an older posi-tivist view of the nature of historical inquiry: that it is simply not the historian's business to give explanations; his concern is only to describe and narrate. Such a view, it might be mentioned, does not usually prevent these same historians from offering perfectly satisfactory explanations in their un-theoretical moments. And the prevalence of explanatory words and expressions in what, in the preface to this book, I called 'ordinary historical writing', would in any case make the view a rather odd one.

It would be rash to try to read a great deal into the re-actions of historians to the model. Practitioners are not always the best theorists about their own practice; and, in any case, the evidence is conflicting. Yet it appears to me highly sus-picious that the model is accepted most readily by those who are admittedly dissatisfied with history as it is at present. Before joining in the demand for a revolution in historical method, it might be wise to insist on a more sustained attempt to show exactly how, and to what extent, the model does, or could, apply to the explanations historians already give. And in addition, it might be prudent to ask whether, if the model were strictly and deliberately applied, anything would be abandoned which is essential to what historians at present accept as explanation. Hempel and Popper have both offered hints and suggestions in this connexion; but it seems to me that a great deal more would need to be said before it could be claimed that a convincing case for the acceptance of cover-ing law theory in history had been made.

[1] *The Englishman and his History*, Cambridge, 1944, p. 138.
[2] *Clio, A Muse*, London, 1930.

3. *A Defence of the Model*

In his recent book *The Nature of Historical Explanation* Mr. Patrick Gardiner has attempted to provide some of the sustained argument which covering law theory would seem to require if it is to make good its claim. Gardiner takes up the problem where Hempel left it; he recognizes the fact that an argument of some subtlety is needed, since it is not at all obvious that the model applies to historical cases. He maintains that it does so, despite appearances to the contrary.

The book is divided into four parts, in the first of which the covering law model is represented as revealing the logical structure of explanations given in both formal scientific inquiry and everyday life. According to Gardiner: "We explain our headaches, our insomnia, our good health, and so forth by correlating them with other happenings like sitting too long in the sun, drinking strong black coffee, and taking regular exercise, which have been observed to accompany the events and states to be explained...."[1] Scientific explanations differ from such common sense ones in requiring "a close structural analysis of the phenomena", and this shows itself in the use of technical concepts beyond the precision of the language of common sense. Yet the difference is only one of degree: "the explanation of the physicist and the explanation of the 'plain man' both depend upon observed correlations in experience."[2]

In Part II Gardiner prepares the ground for the contention that explanations in history are of the same general type, by considering and rejecting some familiar *a priori* objections based on peculiar views of the historian's subject-matter. This very useful discussion is intended to shake up common prejudices and dispose the reader to consider on its merits the positive argument for the model. Of four ways of arguing for 'the autonomy of history' which are thus attacked, three are of particular interest here.[3]

---

[1] Op. cit., p. 5.   [2] Op. cit., p. 24.
[3] The fourth argument is that history is, by definition, concerned with events that are past, and past events cannot be known as present ones can (and, *a fortiori*, cannot be explained)—a view attributed to Oakeshott.

The first is that historical events are unique and hence un-classifiable—a view attributed to Croce. If true, this would rule out the possibility of bringing them under general laws at all, for laws govern types or classes of events. In meeting this objection, Gardiner does not deny that there is a certain point in saying that "the historian concentrates upon the event in its *unique individuality*"; but he does deny that "historical events possess some absolute uniqueness which necessitates their being known and explained in an especial way".[1] Indeed, he regards it as obvious that, since the historian uses language to refer to the events he studies, he does in fact manage to classify them. The *a priori* objection that he cannot do this must therefore be dismissed.

The second objection is that historical events are, or in-volve, thoughts, and thoughts cannot be brought under law—a view attributed to Collingwood. Once again Gardiner admits that the objection has some force, for in history "we view human behaviour not only in its reactive aspects, but also under the aspect of being purposive, calculated, planned".[2] And when we do this, he agrees, we do not look for causes or bring the actions under law. But although "the two forms of explanation are different [and] it is a mistake to try to conflate them", we should not conclude that the giving of a non-causal explanation rules out the giving of a causal or law-covered one. Nor should we allow ourselves to think that the 'insides' of actions which the historian seeks to discover are "queer objects, invisible engines that make the wheels go round". For we understand actions in the non-causal way largely by taking account of overt behaviour, and our proce-dure in giving the explanation (which Gardiner discusses further in Part IV) amounts to subsuming what was done, if not under a 'law', then at least under a 'lawlike' statement: a statement implying that the agent was disposed to do things of a certain sort.

The third objection is that historical events are irreducibly rich and complex, so that, whether there really are any regu-

[1] Op. cit., pp. 40, 42.   [2] Op. cit., p. 47.

larities in them or not, we cannot discern any. This view is
attributed to Fisher, and perhaps also to Bury. And Gardiner
agrees that when we come to consider events like the English,
French, and Russian revolutions, it is tempting to conclude
that "the 'things' or events with which history deals are too
big and unwieldy, too complex and various, to be generalized
about". They seem to "overflow the edges of any precise
classification".[1] But we must not imagine that it is a peculiarity
of the events themselves which thus sets limits to our ability
to generalize. For there is a linguistic side to the problem;
terms like 'revolution', which indicate what it is we are to
generalize about, are "accommodating terms, able to cover a
vast number of events falling within an indefinitely circum-
scribed range".[2] The 'language of historical descriptions'
consequently does not admit of the framing of precise
generalizations. But this is not at all the same as concluding
that historical events cannot be generalized about at all.

Such a summary does scant justice to Gardiner's discussion
of some very common and troublesome opinions about history. Even where the argument itself is rather sketchy, its
approach is often illuminating. Gardiner does not try to *refute*
these various philosophical objections outright; his aim is
rather to show that, taken in an ordinary sense, the propositions which formulate them express truisms about history,
the historian's interests and his problems, and that they
need not be interpreted as setting up metaphysical barriers
against the use of laws in explanation. But he wishes, of
course, to establish more than this negative thesis. The remainder of the book is therefore devoted to showing that the
covering law model *does* function in history—indeed, that it
must do so.

As might be expected, in view of his treatment of the objections noted, Gardiner's positive account goes considerably
beyond Hempel's in making concessions to those who object
to the model as unrealistic. His major departure is in allowing
a second type of explanation, which, far from being 'pseudo',

[1] Op. cit., p. 58.   [2] Op. cit., p. 61.

is perfectly proper when we are concerned with human conduct of a purposive rather than a 'reactive' kind. Having
denied that "an explanation of the form, '*x* did *y* because he
wanted *z*. . .', refers to the existence of a causal relation between
two events", Gardiner goes on to argue that the "function of
the 'because'" in such explanation is to set the agent's action
"within a pattern, the pattern of his normal behaviour".[1] The
particular action is explained in terms of a dispositional characteristic of the agent, and this, he admits, cannot strictly be
regarded as subsuming what was done under a covering
general law.

It seems to me that the departure from the covering law
model here is a major one, both in what it asserts and what it
suggests. Gardiner does, it is true, represent dispositional
explanation as not a very serious falling-away from covering
law respectability. The explanatory statement which attributes
the dispositional characteristic to the agent is at least 'lawlike'.
But although he does not emphasize this, a logical discon-
tinuity is nevertheless recognized in the field of explanation
which other covering law theorists have been most anxious
to avoid. Such an admission can scarcely fail to strip the
model of a little of its pristine, *a priori* plausibility—one of
the barriers to getting serious consideration for alternative
accounts. It invites the question: 'If one, why not many such
logical differences, provided that recognition of them is forced
upon us by a consideration of the way historians' explanations
go?' Gardiner does not explore such possibilities; the dispositional analysis which he gives in Part IV is hurried and
schematic by comparison with his earlier discussion. His
chief concern appears to be to narrow the front which exponents of the model require to defend, and then to set about
defending it.

Yet even in the remaining cases, where a covering law *is*
held to function in any given explanation, Gardiner has much
to add (in Part III) to Hempel's remarks about the 'looseness'
of the law in historical contexts. He points out that "an event

[1] Especially op. cit., pp. 124–5.

in history is frequently not so obviously a case of a given type as is an event treated by science or by common sense".[1] He calls our attention to the fact that the historian's explanatory statement often comes as a kind of summing up, after the real work of the explanation has been done, so that that statement itself, if it is to be properly understood, must be referred back to the details on which it rests.[2] And he maintains that the word 'cause' itself, which appears in so many explanations given by historians, is vague in its own peculiar way. In ordinary life, "to give the cause of an event is to select one from a number of conditions"—notably "that condition which enables us to produce or prevent that event";[3] and in history, too, the word 'cause' has a "contextual reference".

For these and other reasons, the function of covering laws will appear very different in scientific and historical cases. In history, Gardiner warns us, the laws will have a number of 'levels of imprecision'.[4] The historian, as we saw, uses ordinary language; and the component terms of his laws, unlike the concepts of science, are 'loose and porous'. White was thus misguided to look for 'specifically historical terms'; history employs none—not even sociological ones—in the great majority of cases. In addition, there is often a wide *ceteris paribus* clause to be read into the historian's laws, leaving a certain play between law and case. Indeed, when the laws are formulated with sufficient care, it may be found necessary to include in them some such qualifying term as 'usually'; for it is not "implied that they *always* hold". Small wonder then that in history there is "always a risk in moving from the general hypothetical or 'law' to the particular case, the risk that in the particular case factors unknown to us may have been present".[5]

Confronted with Gardiner's analysis, a true positivist might very well say: 'So much the worse for history as it is presently studied'; and he might intensify his demand that the subject be made more 'scientific'. But Gardiner insists that it is a mistake,

---

[1] Op. cit., p. 87.   [2] Op. cit., p. 90.   [3] Op. cit., p. 101.
[4] Op. cit., pp. 93–94.   [5] Op. cit., p. 92.

and damaging to historical writing, to draw too close a parallel
between explanation in history and in the formal sciences.
For we do not always want to talk about the world the way
a physicist does; in history the precision of scientific language
is out of place. The covering law model is no more than a
kind of logical 'marker' or ideal, to which actual explanations
in history can be shown to approximate to a limited degree.
The extent to which they do so depends upon the interests of
historians, and these not only allow, but positively enjoin, a
general looseness of structure of the kind Gardiner explores.
To those who urge that historians speak more precisely, and
thus become more 'scientific', Gardiner recommends the
functional view of language: a view which holds that the only
'right' way of talking is the way which enables the speaker to
get on with the job in hand.

4. *Aim of the Present Discussion*

Gardiner's discussion of the nature of explanation in history seems to me a most useful one. It puts the case for the
covering law model with a moderation clearly induced by a
desire to illuminate what the historian actually does. It candidly admits that the model "may suggest an artificial picture
of what the historian is doing, an over-simplified, too tidy
account".[1] No doubt Gardiner advances far enough beyond
the cruder forms of the theory to produce an analysis which,
in many respects, historians might themselves find illuminating. Yet even in allowing a second type of explanation, he
insists that it, too, is analysable in terms of some kind of
'regularity', and in abandoning the claim that history is
'scientific' in any technical sense, he does not give up, but only
blurs, the logical pattern of explanation which his predecessors
claimed to derive from scientific procedure.

For all his concessions to the peculiarities of historical
practice, I think it is clear that Gardiner remains, in essentials,
a covering law theorist. His modifications of the model, like

[1] Op. cit., p. 88.

those allowed by Popper and Hempel, are all designed to show that, even in the most unlikely cases, the real force or point of the explanations which historians offer is only to be brought out by emphasizing their resemblance to the covering law ideal. There is, of course, nothing necessarily vicious about approaching the subject with the question: 'To what extent do actual explanations in history approximate to the structure of the covering law model?' But the danger of doing this will obviously be that more will sometimes be read into an historical example than is actually there, and, just as unfortunate, that important features which *are* there will pass unnoticed. In spite of his repeated declarations of the historian's right to determine his own way of dealing with his subject-matter, it seems to me that Gardiner has not escaped the dangers of such a procedure.

In the chapters to follow I shall argue that if we are to produce a helpful account of the logic of explanation in history, more is required than a mere 'loosening up' of the covering law model. This model is, in fact, so misleading that it ought to be *abandoned* as a basic account of what it is to give an explanation. This is not to say that no trace of it will be found at all in the explanations historians normally give, for it is an odd philosophical doctrine which can be shown to be completely false. But the traces, I shall argue, are almost always misdescribed. To bring these traces into proper perspective, I shall suggest that we constantly ask ourselves the question: 'What is the point here of saying that a general law has an indispensable function in the explanation given?'

The general course of my argument will be as follows.[1] In Chapter II, I shall investigate the notion of an 'implicit' appeal to law as it is used by covering law theorists; and I shall deny that there *need* be anything properly so-called in an historian's explanation. The discussion of this question will force a reconsideration of the problem of the uniqueness of the

[1] As the above chapter outline will suggest, I try, as far as possible, to discuss various reasons for dissatisfaction with the model independently. Thus failure to be convinced by the argument of any single chapter should not be taken as indicating that the general case against the covering law theory has broken down.

objects of historical study, and of the role of the judgement of the historian in giving an explanation. In Chapter III, I shall go on to ask what should in general be said about cases where a covering law is known, and perhaps even mentioned; and I shall argue that appealing to the law in such cases is not *ipso facto* explaining what falls under it. This argument will direct our attention to the question of the logical type of the term 'explanation'. For it will be an essential part of my general thesis that positivists have wrongly taken it to be a term of formal logic, whereas it is really a pragmatic one. Further light will be thrown on this pragmatic dimension in subsequent chapters.

In Chapter IV, I shall consider the logical structure of specifically causal explanations in history. Besides expanding Gardiner's very useful discussion of the 'contextual reference' of the word 'cause', I shall try to show why knowledge of causal laws is especially irrelevant to the giving of causal explanations; and I shall suggest that it is often the erroneous view of causal analysis which the covering law theory tends to support which lies behind campaigns for the elimination of causal language from historical writing altogether. In Chapter V, I shall turn to the restricted range of explanations—mainly of individual human actions—which Gardiner calls 'noncausal', and for which he offers a dispositional rather than a strictly law-covered analysis. My argument here will be that most of our explanations of such actions are indeed of a special logical type, which I call 'rational', but that the covering law doctrine is especially beside the point when applied to such cases—on both its necessary and sufficient condition interpretations. And the peculiarities of such explanations cannot be brought out by dispositional analysis either, although dispositional explanation, it will be admitted, constitutes a special type whose relation to rational and causal explanations has sometimes been misunderstood.

Finally, in Chapter VI, a type of explanation will be discussed—rather more briefly—which stands quite outside the normal 'Why? Because . . .' pattern, and whose logical structure departs quite radically from the covering law model. Such departures, I shall argue, can only be appreciated if we attend closely to the questions which the explanations concerned may be regarded as answering.

To bring out the nature of my disagreement with Gardiner's modified covering law theory as sharply as possible, I shall from time to time deliberately use examples which he has already discussed. I have no desire, however, to exaggerate the extent of our disagreement, or to deny the obvious debt which my discussion owes to his. And I should like to express substantial agreement with him about the *kind* of inquiry needed. Our concern is with the logic of historical thinking, interpreting 'logic' in the broad sense made familiar by contemporary analytic philosophers. It is not epistemology or psychology, as some opponents of the covering law theory appear to believe. Gardiner, himself, having drawn attention to the historian's use of causal and near-causal expressions, formulates the nature of the task quite satisfactorily in these words: "We must try to discover what in general are the criteria which govern the historian's usage of expressions like these, and under what conditions it is justifiable to say that a 'historical connection' exists between two events or states of affairs."[1] And again: "We must . . . consider what it is that historians are doing when they speak of two events as causally related to one another, and under what conditions it is deemed legitimate in history to say that two facts are connected."[2] Like Gardiner's book, the present discussion endeavours to elicit some of the complicated criteria of 'giving an explanation' accepted and acceptable in historical studies. And it is my contention that covering law theory fails to give them.

[1] Op. cit., p. 70.   [2] Op. cit., pp. 80–81.

II

THE DOCTRINE OF IMPLICIT LAW

1. *Covering Law as a Necessary Condition*

LET me begin by challenging in a general way the claim
that the covering law model, as it is most naturally interpreted, and as its exponents themselves usually represent
it, states a *necessary* condition of giving an explanation of
historical events and conditions. The contention I want to
examine is that an explanation somehow *requires* a law, that it
is not *complete* unless the law in question has been specified,
that it is not *tenable* unless the law has been verified by an
appropriate empirical procedure. My thesis will be that in
spite of there being a certain point in saying of quite ordinary
explanations in history that they require to be covered by laws,
the conclusions which covering law logicians have commonly
gone on to draw are quite unjustified. For although there is
indeed a sense in which a 'law' can often be shown to be 'required' by the kind of explanation the historian gives, it is
usually not the sort of thing that these logicians would find
very interesting. And the only relevant laws which would
interest them are not required in the sense which they intend.[1]

To assess the covering law claim we must discover both the
exact sense in which the alleged law is required—i.e. elucidate
the 'covering' relation—and make clear the logical characteristics of the law itself. Unfortunately, as even the brief survey
of the previous chapter will have shown, the terminology of
covering law literature is rather fluid when these points are
touched upon. It is as if the claim intended could not be put
quite satisfactorily either in technical or ordinary language.

[1] In Chapter VI, I shall argue that for some kinds of explanation in history the
claim that a covering law is a necessary condition of giving the explanation is
totally incorrect. Nor are the points I am prepared to concede in the present
chapter conceded in connexion with the kind of explanation which, in Chapter V,
I shall call 'rational'.

There are, for instance, many ways of speaking of the supposed 'role' of the covering law itself, when an explanation is
given. Mr. R. S. Peters puts the claim in its strongest form
when he declares: "To explain an occurrence is to *deduce* it
from general or lawlike statements, together with initial
condition statements describing particular states of affairs."[1]
But usually something much less than this is asserted; it is
said only that a law is presupposed, or assumed, or taken for
granted in giving the explanation. Even so, there are a number
of not obviously equivalent ways of characterizing what
Hempel calls the 'theoretical function' of the law in question.
According to Popper, for instance, the law is 'tacitly used' in
the explanation; White speaks of a law as 'guiding' an explanation;[2] and although at one point Gardiner declares that an
explanation holds 'by virtue of' a law, at another he says that
in history a covering law only has 'a bearing upon' what falls
under it.[3] If we are to assess the force of the model's claim, on
its necessary condition side, we must try to go beyond such
non-committal ways of characterizing the logical 'role' in
question.

When we come to look at what is said about the covering
law itself, we shall also find a number of quite different terms
used. Thus Hempel, having defined what he means by 'general
law' quite austerely as "a statement of universal conditional
form which is capable of being confirmed or disconfirmed by
suitable empirical findings", goes on to allow that 'probability
hypotheses' based on statistical information will do. Popper
speaks of 'causal laws', 'laws of nature', and 'trivial empirical
generalizations' as if the differences between them did not
much matter for covering law theory. Gardiner refers indis-
criminately to the covering law as a 'generalization', a 'rule',
and a 'general hypothetical'. My argument, both in this and in
later chapters, will endeavour to show that it is only if we take
the differences between such logical characterizations seriously

[1] Op. cit., p. 141. My italics.
[2] Op. cit., p. 225, n. 1.
[3] Op. cit., p. 92.

that we can see clearly whether the model is sound—and, indeed, exactly what its claims are.

There is a possible objection to the line of argument I shall adopt in the present chapter which should perhaps be mentioned at the outset. For it might be urged that although there is considerable uncertainty as to what exactly is meant by a 'general law', it is clear from what at least *some* of the logicians in question have written that they do not intend to restrict the number of laws which may be employed in any particular explanation to *one*. May I not, therefore, beg questions unnecessarily in undertaking to discover what is meant by *the* covering law? Does it not make the model appear unnecessarily ridiculous—a mere 'straw man'—to suppose that we are expected to discern a single law covering the explanation of such complex historical phenomena as, say, the Norman Conquest or the unpopularity of Louis XIV?

Covering law theorists themselves furnish the answer to this objection. For it is notably not just in very simple cases that they speak of a single covering law being required. In the example quoted in Chapter I, Popper suggests that the explanation of the first division of Poland 'tacitly used' a trivial law of the form: "If of two armies which are about equally well-armed and led, one has a tremendous superiority in men, then the other never wins." This is surely exactly the sort of case where one would expect methodological realism to demand that the requirement of a *single* law be dropped. Yet Popper has no hesitation in attempting to find such a single law, the admitted triviality of his candidate being regarded as no barrier to its performance of its explanatory role. The same tendency is also exemplified in Gardiner's discussion;[1] and even Hempel, who formulates his theory carefully in terms of laws, cannot resist adding that the laws and initial condition statements taken together "imply the statement that whenever events of the kind described . . . occur, an event of the kind to be explained will take place". The strong temptation he obviously feels to assimilate the more complex case to the

---

[1] As will appear below in sections 4 and 6.

simple one is part of what we have to investigate. Having investigated it, I shall go on, later, to ask whether my conclusions would have to be modified in any important way if more realistic assumptions, methodologically speaking, were made about the laws said to be 'used'.

One way of getting at exactly what is meant—or, indeed, what *could* be meant—by a covering law would be to ask how an exponent of the model might set about the task of convincing an historian that such laws are indeed required by the explanations he gives. For, as covering law theorists themselves admit, the explanations found in history books seldom mention any laws. Nor are laws any more likely to be mentioned in explicit statements by the historian of how he arrived at the explanations he eventually gives. Is there any way in which the philosopher could convince the historian that laws were nevertheless somehow assumed or 'tacitly used' by the explanations given? To some extent Gardiner and Hempel have already given the covering law logician's answer to this question, but I wish in this chapter to re-examine it. For although I think that Gardiner, in particular, gauges correctly the way a historian would respond to a philosopher's probing, it does not seem to me that this response warrants the covering law conclusions he goes on to draw.

2. *Loose Laws and Probability Hypotheses*

Let us suppose that an historian makes a statement like: 'Louis XIV died unpopular because he pursued policies detrimental to French national interests'—an example which Gardiner discusses at length. How might a covering law theorist set about vindicating his claim that there is a law implicit in the explanation?

Two related, although quite different, arguments are commonly used in covering law literature. It will sometimes, for instance, be contended that although the historian mentions no laws in the explanation he gives, and although he may not have formulated any in arriving at the conclusion that it is tenable, still, if the explanation were challenged in a certain way, he would have to fall back on a law if he wanted to defend it. Thus Gardiner, at one point, observes:

> . . . whenever a causal *explanation* is doubted or queried (as opposed to the doubting or querying of the truth value of one of its limbs) it is the generalization that warrants its utterance which comes under fire, and the same generalization must be defended by reference to previous experience if the claim to have offered a satisfactory explanation is to be upheld. In this sense it may be correct to speak of an 'implicit' reference to generalizations in all explanations.[1]

This argument is an important one, and I shall return to it in a later section of this chapter. But there is another, particularly neat and apparently conclusive one which it might be well to consider first: the claim that the explanation given requires a law in a *logical* rather than methodological sense of 'requires'. The word 'because', and the many substitute expressions for it which are to be found in the historian's explanations, will be said to depend for their very *meaning* on some kind of related general statement. No doubt an historian who gives an explanation like the one cited above will deny that he even knows a relevant law. But if the logician's argument can be sustained, it will, of course, be useless for the historian to object that his explanation instantiates no covering law. For what he says in giving the explanation will in some sense *commit* him to the truth of some corresponding general statement, so that if the latter cannot stand, neither can the explanation. The fact that an historian who uses an explanatory statement like the one mentioned does not realize that its truth depends on the truth of a law will be represented as a fact to be deplored, not one to make the starting-point of a methodology. People are all too seldom clearly aware of the full implications of what they say, and it may be presumed to be part of the logician's job to bring such lapses to our notice.

What is the nature of this allegedly 'tight' logical connexion? Some philosophers take the tough-minded view that an explanation *entails* its corresponding law.[2] Hempel very nearly

---

[1] Op. cit., pp. 25–26.

[2] This claim should be distinguished from the claim, noted in the preceding section, that the statement that an explained event occurred is entailed by its

makes this claim when he says, of a statement of the form: 'The explanation of C is E', that it "amounts to the statement that, according to certain general laws, a set of events of the kinds mentioned is regularly accompanied by an event of kind E".[1] And Gardiner, too, comes close to it when, at one point, he says that an explanation "entails a reference" to laws.[2]

Now 'entailment' is a term of art which has undergone many vicissitudes in the philosophical journals in recent years. But it is at any rate one common view, especially among logicians who tend to accept the covering law model, that entailment is to be regarded as a relation between two statements such that if 'p' is true, and 'p' entails 'q', then 'q' is true by virtue of some kind of linguistic guarantee. An example of such a logical relation would be: 'This is a cow' entails 'This is a mammal'. Such a relation is spoken of as 'linguistically guaranteed' because it depends on accepted definitions of the terms involved, i.e. 'cow' and 'mammal'. Given these, the entailment obtains; without them it does not. But it is surely very unplausible to claim that a statement of the form: 'E because C', formally entails a law in this fashion. For it would depend on our being able to indicate an accepted criterion or definition of 'because' such that by substitution we could transform the particular statement—the explanation—into a general one—the law. To speak of a linguistic guarantee here would be to beg the question by recommending a definition of 'because' which does not exist—unless, perhaps, in a philosophical dictionary written by a covering law logician.

Exponents of the model may object to such a formal interpretation of entailment; they may object that although this is what has often been meant by 'entails', the term has also been used to designate a non-formal, yet completely 'tight', relation. Mr. R. M. Hare, for instance, defines entailment very broadly thus: "A sentence p entails a sentence q if and only if the fact that a person assents to p but dissents from q is a sufficient

covering law together with statements of the relevant antecedent conditions. The present claim is that from an explanation a covering law can be deduced, not that from a covering law an explanation can be deduced.

[1] See Chapter I, section 1.   [2] Op. cit., p. 30.

criterion for saying that he has misunderstood one or other of the sentences."[1] That is, we might say that an explanation entails a law in the sense that it would be *unintelligible* for anyone to assert the first and deny the second: a person cannot *mean* anything by the explanation if he denies the law. But how could the logician hope to convince the historian of this? The historian has denied that he arrived at his explanation by means of a law; he would—as will appear more clearly later—deny that he would in practice have to defend it by citing a law; could he not also deny that there is any law which, having given the explanation, he would have to accept as true or be convicted of talking nonsense?

The attempt to show the historian that there is some law to which his explanation has indeed committed him often leads exponents of the model into formulating the sort of thing that Popper, in the passage quoted in the preceding section, called a "law of the sociology of military power"; and in the present instance it might produce a candidate like: 'Rulers who ignore their subjects' interests become unpopular.' It is in this way, for instance, that Hempel deals with an explanation of the migration of Dust Bowl farmers to California in terms of drought and sandstorms.[2] Realizing that an historian who gave such an explanation would certainly refuse to stand committed to anything as specific as, say, 'Farmers will always leave dry land when damper areas are accessible', we find Hempel cutting into the hierarchy of possible covering laws at a much higher level of generality with: 'Populations will tend to migrate to regions which offer better living conditions.' Yet it would still be open to a conscientious historian to object that the explanation has not committed him even to this, and the logician would then have to soar to still greater heights of generality. The higher the altitude the more innocuous the covering law becomes from a methodological point of view, and we are bound to wonder what point is served by insisting

---

[1] *The Language of Morals*, Oxford, 1952, p. 25. Hare uses this criterion to support his argument that 'ought' statements entail imperatives.
[2] Op. cit., p. 464.

that the historian has committed himself to anything whatever. Popper calls such laws 'trivial', but it is worth remarking
that their triviality does not depend only on the fact that they
are common knowledge, so that, as he puts it, "we take them
for granted, instead of making conscious use of them". They
are not like, 'If a man jumps over a 400-foot cliff he will dash
his brains out at the bottom'. Their triviality lies in the fact
that the farther the generalizing process is taken, the harder
it becomes to conceive of anything which the truth of the law
would rule out.

If the candidate law ascends too far into generalities it loses
its methodological interest; but if it descends from the strato-
sphere it becomes possible to deny it without withdrawing the
explanation. In the face of such a difficulty, covering law
theorists often employ more cautious substitutes for 'entailment', which suggest its advantages without laying their claim
open to strict test. Thus Gardiner, at one point, says only that
an explanation "implies the formulation of laws or generalizations";[1] and according to Hempel, in historical cases the explanation often merely "points towards" a covering law. If the
use of such terms is intended to mean no more than that a
covering law is *suggested* by an explanation—i.e. to admit that
there is no tight logical connexion at all—it would be difficult
to quarrel with the logician's claim. Indeed, it would seem that
the number of laws suggested by a 'because' statement is quite
embarrassingly large. But the cost of modifying the covering
law claim in this way would surely be rather high; for an
explanation can scarcely be said to stand or fall by what it
suggests. Such a 'loosening up' of the model would be much
more radical than the concession made earlier that an explanatory statement, although it must be *deducible* from its
covering law and antecedent condition statements, need not,
in practice, actually be *deduced* from them.

If important methodological conclusions are to be drawn
from the argument from meaning, the assertion of a tight
logical connexion between law and explanation would seem

[1] Op. cit., p. 5.

to be essential. So the occasional use of 'entails', although it may sometimes be a slip, is not an insignificant one. That Gardiner and Popper, in spite of their avoidance of this term on the whole, really want to *mean* it, is strongly suggested by their willingness to accept in the covering role a law which is tightly connected with its case, even at the cost of allowing the law, rather than the connexion, to be loose.

For there are, of course, two ways in which an exponent of the model could attempt to deal with the difficulty, while refusing to loosen the *specification* of his candidate law. He might, on the one hand, claim that the law which he formulates out of the historian's explanatory statement is strictly entailed by it (although perhaps non-formally); then, in order to ease the historian's misgivings about acknowledging that he is committed to the precise law presented for his inspection, he might concede that the latter contains some such qualification as 'usually'. On the other hand, he might say that, although the elicited law must be regarded as strictly universal in form, it is only loosely connected logically with the explanation which it covers—so that the explanation is not necessarily falsified if the law is shown to be untrue. The same covering law theorists can be found adopting both of these expedients at different points in their writings. And Hempel appears to have settled uneasily on the ground between them when he remarks that "in many cases, the content of the hypotheses which are tacitly assumed in a given explanation can be reconstructed only quite approximately".[1] The impression given is that, although the laws concerned are both universal in form and tightly connected with the explanations falling under them, it is unfortunately impossible to say what they are.

Usually, in the desire to achieve a position which is both plausible to the historian and methodologically positive, covering law theorists are prepared to mutilate the law rather than the connexion. Thus, as we have seen, Hempel sometimes says that the covering function may be performed by a 'probability hypothesis'; and Gardiner discovers in the laws required by

[1] Op. cit., p. 464.

the historian's explanations a number of "levels of imprecision". In science we are thought to have genuinely universal
laws of the form: 'Whenever *C* then *E*'; in history we have
to make do with laws which would have to be expressed:
'Whenever *C* then probably *E*', or 'Whenever *C* then usually
E'.[1] This unfortunate lack of rigour will be accounted for in
different ways by different theorists. Whatever its source, it
is assumed to account for the fact that historians mistakenly
think their explanations entail no laws at all.

Yet the view that the historian's explanation derives its
force and point from some less-than-universal law, although
perhaps the lesser of two evils, is surely highly unsatisfactory
from the standpoint of the covering law theorist himself. The
mutilation of the alleged law does, it is true, make it more
difficult for the historian to repudiate any particular candidate,
yet it does not make it impossible. It is still open to him to
make nonsense out of the claim that he is logically committed
to anything of importance by insisting that the qualification
of the law be increased from 'usually' to 'often', or from 'often'
to 'sometimes'. And even if the historian accepted a loose
law as undeniable, having given his explanation, this would
scarcely vindicate the full covering law claim. For the question
would surely then arise whether such a law would actually
explain the cases to which it is represented as applying. Does
the 'law', 'Whenever *C* then usually *E*', really explain the fact
that *in this case* an *E* followed a *C*? Would not the *same* 'law'
have 'explained', in the same sense, the non-occurrence of an
E as well? It seems to me that whether or not such a law
would explain a general fact—e.g. that we have more often
found *E* following *C* than not—its explanatory force does not
extend to particular occurrences falling under it.

3. *The Law Implicit in Complete Explanation*

The covering law theorist thus finds himself on the horns
of a dilemma. If he loosens the connexion between law and
explanation, the law said to give the explanation its force is

[1] See Note A, p. 170.

not logically required. But if he loosens the law itself, it be-comes questionable whether what is logically required really has explanatory force. If any sort of case is to be made for covering law theory in historical contexts, some further ac-count will obviously have to be given of such a puzzling state of affairs.

In the face of such difficulties, the logician may shift his ground a little. For he may argue that his failure to elicit from the historian's explanatory statement a covering law which is both plausible and methodologically interesting arises out of the fact that the explanations found in history books are generally incomplete. To say, for instance, that Louis XIV died unpopular because of his pursuit of policies detrimental to French interests, is only to make a beginning of explaining the king's unpopularity—it is, perhaps, what Hempel would call a mere 'explanation sketch'. The historian would ob-viously have to take into account much more than this before he could represent his explanation as providing information from which a *prediction* of that unpopularity could have been attempted. And, as most covering law theorists are careful to insist, explanation and prediction are, on their theory, correlative operations.[1]

Would the reformulation of the model as a theory of *com-plete* explanation make it more acceptable to historians? At the outset, perhaps not; for it may very well seem to them that if a complete explanation is one which represents what happened as predictable from a set of 'sufficient conditions', exponents of the model will find themselves claiming to elucidate the logical structure of something which is neither achieved nor attempted in their subject. Yet most historians would prob-ably allow that some explanations may be regarded as more complete than others; and they might find it difficult to deny

---

[1] See, e.g. Hempel, op. cit., p. 462. As will appear in Chapter III, I do not think that explanation and prediction *are* correlative in this way; and as Chapter IV will show, there are reasons, too, for disputing the suggestion that the his-torian's original explanation was incomplete, in view of the question it may be presumed to be answering. But I let these points pass here for the sake of argu-ment.

that the criterion which would be applied in deciding between them would be the degree to which each approximated to the logician's ideal. Are we to conclude, then, that the failure of the model to apply exactly to historical cases is due only to the fact that historians' explanations are always incomplete?

We shall, I think, be in a better position to deal with this question if we ask how the logician might attempt to convince the historian that, in some way which vindicates the revised covering law claim, a complete explanation might, on occasion, be given. And this the logician might attempt to do by adopting a rather different procedure from the one envisaged in the preceding section when the historian refuses to accept his candidate for the role of covering law. For instead of attempting to meet the latter's objections by making the antecedent clause of the law more and more general, or by loosening either the law or the connexion, he might have adopted the alternative of trying to induce the historian to modify the explanation itself.

Let us suppose that, having given his explanation of Louis XIV's unpopularity, the historian denies that he has committed himself to the law: 'Rulers who pursue policies detrimental to their subjects' interests become unpopular.' And let us suppose that the logician then insists on bringing to light exactly *why* the historian refuses to stand committed to the law. As Gardiner has suggested, the latter would probably object that, in giving the explanation he did, it was not his intention to imply that *any* policies which were detrimental to a country's interests would make their rulers unpopular. It was because such policies took the peculiar form they did in this particular case that they can be regarded as providing the explanation—e.g. the involvement of the country in foreign wars, the persecution of religious minorities, the maintenance of a parasitic court, and so on. But the logician, in the face of this objection, might simply agree to absorb the historian's specification of the king's policies into his law, which would be reformulated as: 'Rulers who involve their countries in foreign wars, who persecute religious minorities, and who maintain parasitic courts, become unpopular.' And although the historian may still have some qualms about saying that this would in general be true, the logician might offer to absorb any further objections in the same way, no matter how exactly the historian felt obliged to characterize the policies in question.

The latter might, of course, object to the generalization of his explanatory statement on different grounds; for even if the king's policies are eventually specified to his satisfaction, there remains the possibility that in circumstances unlike those of the late seventeenth century in France, the pursuit of policies specifiable in the same way would not lead to unpopularity. The fact that they did in Louis's case might depend in addition on the fact that at least some of the policies in question were unsuccessful; that they were obviously attributable to the king himself, and so on. And besides such additional positive conditions, the explanation might not be regarded as complete without taking some negative ones into account; for the effect of the policies specified would depend, too, on the fact that Louis failed to head off his unpopularity in various ways—for instance, by a policy of 'bread and circuses'. But the logician might insist that there is nothing in his theory which prevents his taking all these additional factors, both positive and negative, into account, and he could continue the revision of his law in such a fashion as: 'Rulers who . . . and who are regarded as the true authors of their policies, and who do not offer "bread and circuses" become unpopular.' If the historian still rejects the suggestion that he commits himself to the assertion that this would always be true, the dialectical pattern of suggestion, objection, and revision has been sketched by means of which any specific further objection could be absorbed into the logician's law.[1]

What conclusions should be drawn about the covering law claim in view of the possibility of such a dialectic developing

---

[1] Mr. J. R. Lucas uses a similar dialectic to bring out features of moral arguments, in 'The Lesbian Rule', *Philosophy*, 1955, pp. 195–213. Lucas regards this as a typical pattern of argument throughout the humanities.

between logician and historian? Covering law theorists will no doubt say that what the dialectic elicits is a set of sufficient conditions falling under a covering law; for at every stage, the logician's revision answers the historian's objection that what the law sets out need not be universally true. But opponents of the model may very well insist that the series of more and more precise laws which the historian's objections force upon the logician is an *indefinite* one. And I think it is true that, in an important sense of 'need', the historian, having given his explanation, *need not* accept any particular candidate the logician formulates. It is always *logically* possible for the explanation to be just out of reach every time the logician's pincers snap shut. To this extent, the logician's argument from meaning still remains inconclusive; for the conjunction of an explanatory statement and the denial of any law that might be suggested, is never self-contradictory, or even strictly unintelligible. To put it another way: no matter how complicated the expression with which we complete a statement of the form, '*E* because . . .', it is part of the 'logic' of such 'because' statements that additions to the explanatory clause are never ruled out by our acceptance of the original statement.

To regard such an argument as entirely disposing of the revised covering law claim, however, is surely a little frivolous. For as the set of conditions which the historian's objections and qualifications fills out becomes more complicated, it will at any rate become harder and harder for the historian to deny that from such a set the unpopularity of a ruler could have been *predicted*. At some point or other in the dialectical progress, the reasons which the historian will be able to offer for refusing to accept the covering law will begin to appear rather thin; it will become not only irritating, but unreasonable, to suggest that there was any practical possibility of unpopularity not occurring in a situation like the one characterized, whatever else might happen to be the case. Unless he fortifies himself with a metaphysical theory to the effect that everything is relevant to everything else, there would seem to be *practical* limits to the sort of argument which the historian could use to escape the logical pincers of the argument from meaning in its present, weaker form.

In addition, the covering law logician might contend that although he cannot show that any of the specific laws he formulates are *logically* required by the historian's explanations, there is nevertheless *some* general law which *is* logically required. For the historian would appear to be logically committed at least to the 'law': 'Any ruler pursuing policies and in circumstances exactly like those of Louis XIV would become unpopular.' Such a general 'law' is, no doubt, no more than a vacuous limiting case of a covering law. It is so odd in several ways that it is probably misleading to call it a law at all. It cannot be formulated without mentioning particular things; it is required not only by the specific explanation under examination, but by *any* explanation of Louis's unpopularity in terms of his policies and circumstances; it could be of no methodological interest, since the use of the word 'exactly' in effect rules out the possibility which calling it a 'law' at first seems to envisage. Yet the eliciting of such a vacuous 'law' does show that the argument from meaning—the conviction that some sort of generality was logically involved in the original explanation—was not entirely an illusion.

And the logician might, perhaps, go on to claim that what the dialectic between logician and historian does is provide such a vacuous 'law' with content. For the notion of 'exactly the same policies and circumstances' is one which has no meaning for any actual inquiry; it is enough for the purpose of the formulation of laws, and of prediction in accordance with them, that two situations resemble each other in *relevant* respects. What the dialectic does is *formulate* the respects in which another situation must resemble the one under examination for the same explanation to hold good.

It is important to add, however, that even if the historian concedes the point, a tightly connected and universal law could still not be extracted from his explanation—now 'complete' in the sense indicated—without still another concession being made. For the framing of a general law into which the elicited conditions are to be incorporated as antecedent may encounter a further difficulty in the fact that at least some of these conditions will probably have been stated by the historian in particular rather than general terms. The historian who specifies what he takes note of in arriving at the detailed explanation of Louis XIV's unpopularity, will mention not only universals like 'warlike foreign policy', but also particulars like 'attacks on the Jansenists'. In the sketch I gave of the dialectic between logician and historian, this difficulty was deliberately avoided in the hope of making the quite different problem of the sufficiency of the historian's conditions clear. But, as Hempel very properly emphasizes in his formal statement of the model, it is universals, not particulars, which are "the object of description and explanation in every branch of empirical science"; and he leaves us in no doubt that 'E' and '$C_1 \ldots C_n$' in his schema stand for kinds of events, not particular happenings.

The fact that the historian, in mentioning, for example, 'attacks on the Jansenists', does not say in virtue of what general characteristic he regards these as a reason for expecting unpopularity, leaves open the possibility of a regress similar to the one already stopped. If we are to advance from the historian's statement of explanatory conditions to the assertion of a 'general hypothetical', it will therefore be necessary for the logician once again to require the historian to be 'reasonable'; he will have to obtain the admission that it is attacks on the Jansenists because, say, they are *a religious body* that we can regard them as conditions of the king's unpopularity. Only if this is obtained can a covering law be framed which gets rid of the name and definite article altogether. And there is, of course, no more logical compulsion about this transformation than there was about the acceptance of a definite set of conditions as sufficient.

4. *Generalizations and Principles of Inference*

Let us suppose that the historian concedes the rational force of the logician's demands. Then we might say that, having considered and made explicit all the aspects of French interests, royal policy and other things considered relevant (i.e. required for the prediction of such a result), and having phrased them in universal terms, there is a general statement which the historian could not reasonably deny, namely: "Any people *like the French in the aspects specified* would dislike a ruler *like Louis in the respects specified.*" Such a law is not vacuous since the dialectic between logician and historian will have provided us with a definite 'filler' for the expressions italicized.

Does this amount to accepting the covering law theory in the form it takes toward the end of Gardiner's book, where the historian's specification of a detailed set of 'factors' is said "to satisfy the antecedent of a general hypothetical"—whether the historian realizes this or not?[1] Does the argument from meaning succeed after all, provided the logician, instead of loosening the rather simple law he might extract out of the original explanation, induces the historian to round out the explanation itself? I have, in fact, allowed the logician's demands upon the historian without further argument in order to show that even if these *are* conceded, the conclusions generally drawn by covering law theorists—particularly conclusions of a methodological sort—do not necessarily follow. For even if we admit that, having given the 'complete' explanation, it is no longer possible to deny a covering general hypothetical statement of the form, 'If $C_1 \ldots C_n$ then E', it should be recognized that the statement in question, having regard to the way it has been elicited, is scarcely the sort of 'general law' which would satisfy covering law theorists who insist that history become 'scientific'. Upon closer examination, I think it will be found not to be the sort of thing which could be 'appealed to', or 'used', or have a 'theoretical function' in the explanation given—indeed, that it is better called by another name if we wish to avoid being misled by the methodological recommendations which generally go with covering law theory.

[1] Op. cit., p. 97.

One difference between the present entailed 'law' and the one suggested by Popper is obvious. Whereas Popper's 'trivial' law was so vague and general as to be scarcely deniable, the present law is, by contrast, so highly specified that I have made no attempt to write it out. White, alone among covering law logicians, seems to have been uneasy about this. "I do not agree", he writes, "that the causal law implicit in the connections between historical statements are always so trivial that they are not mentioned explicitly; indeed, I think that the failure to mention them is just as often a result of their being too complicated and difficult to state."[1] Yet this reflection does not lead White to the conclusion which appears to me to be warranted: that such a candidate for the covering role is as trivial as Popper's, although trivial in a different way. To put it shortly, it is, or very well may be, a 'law' with only a single case.

This should not be surprising in view of the way the 'law' was elicited from the historian's statement of sufficient conditions. It was elicited simply by means of the demand that the historian be consistent. The logician's claim is really that since the historian agrees that it was because of the presence of a set of factors of type '$C_1 \ldots C_n$' that unpopularity resulted in this particular case—and only because of these—it must follow that unpopularity would always result from such a set of factors. By offering the 'complete' explanation, 'E because $C_1 \ldots C_n$', the historian thus commits himself to the truth of the covering general statement, 'If $C_1 \ldots C_n$ then E'. But what is the logical status of the statement thus elicited? How should it be characterized? It is surely nothing more than a formulation of the *principle of the historian's inference* when he says that from the set of factors specified, a result of this kind could reasonably be predicted. The historian's inference may be said to be *in accordance with* this principle. But it is quite another matter to say that his explanation entails a corresponding *empirical law*.

[1] 'Towards an Analytic Philosophy of History', in M. Farber, ed., *Philosophic Thought in France and the United States*, New York, 1950, p. 720, n. 22.

For our ordinary notion of an 'empirical law' has 'other cases' built right into it. When Hempel formulates the model's requirements in terms of 'universal hypotheses', for instance, he assures us that the latter imply that "whenever events of the kind described in the first group occur, an event of the kind to be explained will take place".[1] When he says that explanation is 'pseudo' unless implicit universal hypotheses can be confirmed "by suitable empirical findings", it is therefore natural to assume that this means experience of other cases similar enough to fall under the same classification as the one under examination. This implication is even more obvious when we speak of empirical *generalizations*—as Gardiner does throughout his discussion of the covering law claim.[2] For the notion of a generalization with but a single case would ordinarily, I think, be regarded as a self-contradictory one. It is thus interesting to note that when Gardiner applies the doctrine of implicit law to a particularly complicated and detailed historical example, the term 'generalization' suddenly, and without explanation, drops out of use, to be supplanted by the more formal 'general hypothetical'.

Reference to a law as a 'general hypothetical' is a logician's way of talking. The point of such terminology is put by Professor G. Ryle in a general discussion of the relation of statements of the form 'if *p* then *q*' to corresponding arguments ('*p* so *q*') and explanations ('*q* because *p*').[3] Knowing the truth of a general hypothetical, Ryle contends, is simply knowing how to argue and explain in accordance with it. The hypothetical is a statement, but what it states is the principle implicit in those arguments and explanations which are said to apply it. It tells us nothing about what is, has been, or will be the case; it tells us only what we should be able to say *if* so-and-so were the case. To assert the truth of 'if *p* then *q*' is to claim to be justified in inferring 'so *q*' if we notice *p*, or 'because *p*' if we notice *q* and *p*. The hypothetical belongs to

[1] See Chapter I, section 1.
[2] See, for instance, op. cit., pp. 84, 85, 87, 89, 93, 94, 97, 98.
[3] In ' "If", "So" and "Because" ', in M. Black, ed., *Philosophical Analysis*, Ithaca, N.Y., 1950, pp. 323–40.

the language of reasoning—of norms and standards, not of facts and descriptions.

Ryle speaks of 'if p then q' as an *inference license*; for he regards it as exhibiting our license to infer or explain in corresponding ways. But, as he does not mention, the hypothetical statement, unlike the licenses issued by the civil authorities, does not show the *source* of its authority on its face. It reveals nothing about the way it came to be issued; in particular, it does not indicate that its justification lies in the fact that whenever we have found 'p' to be true, we have found 'q' to be true as well. Thus to claim simply that a 'general hypothetical' lurks implicitly in the historian's explanation is to claim considerably less than covering law theorists generally do when they formulate their model in ordinary language. For if the logician's statement 'if p then q', is to be understood in conjunction with the rubric, 'we can infer that . . .', rather than 'we have found that . . .', to say that the historian's explanation commits him to the covering 'law' is merely to say that it commits him, in consistency, to reasoning in a similar way in any further cases which may turn up, since he claims universal validity for the corresponding argument, 'p so q'.

The distinction thus drawn between two interpretations which can be placed upon the notion of a 'covering law'— indeed, between two ways of interpreting the hypothetical statement, 'if p then q'—is not just logic-chopping; for it helps to clarify the positions of both opponents and supporters of the covering law model. On the one hand, it helps to explain the (quite justifiable) hesitation of the historian to admit that his explanation commits him to anything which he would recognize as a *law*. He may have no reason to believe that the incredibly complex concatenation of circumstances which is symbolized as 'p' will ever recur. How then can he assent to the generalization, 'if (i.e. *whenever*) p then q'? Hence, perhaps, the increased persuasiveness of the logician's hypothetical if it is formulated in its subjunctive (i.e. non-existential) form: 'If there had been, or were to be, p, then there would have been, or would be, q.' To this the historian will probably be

less inclined to object, although he may think it a rather useless piece of 'speculation'.

Distinguishing between empirical laws and principles of
inference also helps to explain how the logician could remain
so firmly convinced that, despite the historian's reluctance to
agree, the explanation *must* exhibit the pattern set forth in the
model. For the logician will regard it as obvious that every
rational argument must have a principle—a kind of covert
universality which is brought out by what I have called the
demand for consistency. And this principle can be stated by
means of a hypothetical statement—a 'general law'. From the
vantage-point of abstract logical analysis, it is not immediately
obvious how misleading it can be to draw the conclusion that
a valid explanation entails a covering law, without specifying
more clearly what 'law' is to mean. The need to make a distinction between general statements which express empirical
generalizations and those which merely project in general
terms the argument of the historian in a particular case may
perhaps be obscured, too, by the fact that in *some* cases
covering empirical laws may be explicitly mentioned in giving
explanations. For in such cases, a failure to distinguish between
'empirical law' and 'inference license' would cause no confusion.

It is the methodological remarks which often accompany
statements of covering law theory which show most clearly
the need to make distinctions of the kind drawn above. For
the legitimate, but thin, logical truth in the doctrine of implicit law is often perverted when its implications for historical
practice come to be drawn. Thus White, in a carefully argued
article, represents the historian's explanatory problem as the
finding of true statements satisfying the antecedents of known
laws, with previously known historical facts as consequents.[1]
The suggestion seems to be that the success of explanation in
history depends on the historian's having a sufficient stock
of preformulated, empirically validated laws on hand—like
methodological spanners which can be used to get a grip on

---

[1] White, op. cit., pp. 718–19.

events of various shapes and sizes as they are encountered. But, as the discussion of the attempts to elicit a complete explanation of Louis XIV's unpopularity suggests, the historian may not find himself confronted with 'standard sizes'.

Even from Hempel's formal statement of the model it is far too easy to draw a questionable methodological moral. Crawford, for instance, concludes from it that since historians actually give explanations "implicitly presupposing statements of law", we must hasten to establish the validity of these laws "by a procedure properly called scientific".[1] Empirical testing cannot begin, he points out, until the general laws in question are deliberately made explicit. To hammer this point home to historians, he admits, is "the main goal" of his argument. But such a methodological recommendation could scarcely survive, without serious modification, an understanding of the argument presented above. For in typical historical cases, the evidence which could be assembled for 'law' and case may coincide.

The misconstruction placed upon the logical truth behind the doctrine of implicit law is also exemplified in attempts to elucidate the logical structure of explanation in terms of the notions 'regularity', 'sequence', or 'instance'. Hempel himself uses these terms in the discussion which follows his original, formal statement of the logical ideal; the relevant law, he observes, "may be assumed to assert a regularity". Hempel's example is followed by Crawford, who, in attacking Mandelbaum, denies that we can speak of determining relations between events "unless we assume that the particular relationships are instances of regular relationships, that is, of regularities that could be formulated as laws". And again (although this is said to be a crude statement of the point): ". . . when we state that something, A, explains the event B, we assume that A is connected with B in some regular sequence."[2] Gardiner, in a cautious moment, asserts only that explanation "may be analysed in terms of regularity".[3] But caution is thrown to the winds when, at another point, he asks: "If our

[1] Op. cit., pp. 155, 165.   [2] Op. cit., pp. 164-5.   [3] Op. cit., pp. 82, 85.

knowledge of the existence of a causal connection is not dependent on our having observed a regularity in the concurrence of two events, we must ask in what instead it can be said to consist"—the question intending to reduce to absurdity any alternative to the covering law answer.

There is nothing in the 'covert universality' of an explanatory statement, in either a complete or incomplete form, which justifies this way of talking. The candidate 'law', the 'regularity', which has been elicited from the historian's explanation is no more than a logician's ghost of the inference actually drawn by the historian, with no immediate methodological implications. There is no point in saying that it is *used*, or *functions*, in the explanation; and there is no point in asserting it except to register one's belief that the inference drawn was a reasonable one. The thesis of the covering law theorist could be stated thus: 'We are not justified in inferring q from p unless "if p then q".' But in view of the licensing status of the hypothetical, this reduces to: 'We are not justified in inferring q from p unless we are justified in inferring q from p.' *Requires the truth of* is just a shadow of *requires the support of*; there is no methodological substance in it.

5. *The Uniqueness of Historical Events*

The conclusion to which we have been forced by the dialectic between logician and historian is that the historian's explanation, when specified in detail, may be found to contain the description of a situation or state of affairs which is *unique*. The argument does not show that this *must* be so, but it shows how easily it might be, and it strongly suggests that, in quite typical cases, it would be.

The claim that historical events and conditions are unique has, of course, often been made, especially by idealist philosophers of history. And it has been attacked as either incorrect or unimportant by most of the covering law theorists who have been mentioned so far. In the form in which they attack it, the claim often arises out of a metaphysical view of the world as composed of radically dissimilar particulars. The view is not easy to state clearly, and it sometimes tricks its exponents into uttering tautologies of the form: 'Everything is the way it is, and not otherwise.' A more acceptable way of putting it would be to say that any actual thing or occurrence you care to select for study is unique in the sense that there is nothing else exactly like it. According to many philosophers who use the argument, this fact raises no insuperable difficulty for scientific inquiry, since the sciences are concerned with abstractions—mere ideal constructions. But history is different in that it seeks to describe and explain what actually happened in all its concrete detail. It therefore follows *a priori* that since laws govern classes or types of things, and historical events are unique, it is not possible for the historian to explain his subject-matter by means of covering laws. If he is to understand it at all, it will have to be by some kind of special insight into particular connexions.

In dealing with this argument, it is not necessary to deny that historical events *are* unique in the sense indicated. Hempel himself, putting it another and perhaps more illuminating way, admits that we can study various aspects or characteristics of anything, and that there is no limit to the number of them we can insist on taking into account. Because of this, a complete description (theoretically speaking) is impossible, and, *a fortiori*, "it is impossible to explain an individual event in the sense of accounting for *all* its characteristics by means of universal hypotheses . . .".[1] Hempel thus converts the idealist argument into a dilemma: either we cannot account for all the characteristics of a thing in explaining it, or we cannot explain it at all because we insist on taking, or trying to take, all of them into account. The covering law theorist naturally prefers to accept the first horn.

Gardiner pushes the criticism of the idealist argument a stage farther. He points out that although the number of aspects of a thing are in theory limitless, we do, in practice, manage without too much difficulty to classify events and things as falling into types or kinds, in spite of the supposedly

[1] Op. cit., p. 461.

irreducible differences between them. And the historian does this as well as the scientist or plain man, as his use of *language* shows; for he uses general terms like 'revolution' and 'conquest', which he could not do if he took the absolute uniqueness view seriously. "The Norman Conquest", Gardiner observes, "was unique in the sense that it occurred at a particular time and place, but it was not unique in the sense that events like it, the invasion of one country by another, for instance, have not occurred on several occasions throughout history."[1] Calling it a conquest at all registers our awareness of this likeness. The historian may say that he concentrates on his events in their 'unique individuality', but we must not conclude from this that such uniqueness "excludes the possibility of their being generalized about in any way".

This argument, which is a popular one among covering law theorists,[2] is sound as far as it goes. But it is important to recognize the limited degree to which it supports the full-blooded counter-claim, and the extent to which it may lead to misunderstandings of the structure of typical explanations in history. For although the classification of a case is a necessary preliminary to bringing it under a general law, it is not itself that 'bringing under law'. Showing that there is no metaphysical barrier to bringing historical events under laws is not the same as showing that the laws are in fact used, or that they are in practice available, or that they must function in the covering law way. Gardiner's argument here is entirely negative; it merely rebuts an ill-advised objection to his thesis. It is possible, of course, that no covering law theorist has thought that such an argument from the use of universal classificatory terms in itself establishes the covering law claim, but the impression given is often to the contrary. In Gardiner's discussion of the Norman Conquest, for instance, it seems to be suggested that the explicability of the Conquest is dependent on there having been other "invasions of one

[1] Op. cit., p. 43.
[2] Versions of it can be found in Hempel, op. cit., p. 461; Mandelbaum, 'Causal Analysis in History', *Journal of the History of Ideas*, 1942, pp. 31–32; M. Cohen, 'Causation, and its Application to History', ibid., p. 21.

country by another", and (should we conclude?) a covering explanatory generalization elicited from the course which they all ran.

Furthermore, although covering law theorists are right to insist that, even if an event is, strictly speaking, absolutely unique, it cannot be explained *as* absolutely unique (where this means explaining *all* of its indefinite number of features), to regard this as disposing of the uniqueness claim is to miss a legitimate interpretation of it, and thereby to miss an important peculiarity of historical inquiry. For (as Gardiner himself admits) we can interpret 'unique' in a relative rather than absolute sense: the sense in which we ordinarily call persons and things unique, meaning that they are peculiar in certain respects. Historical events and conditions are often unique simply in the sense of being different from others with *which it would be natural to group them under a classification term*— and different in ways which interest historians when they come to give their explanations.

Let me illustrate my point. The French Revolution is *a* revolution; that is, it is sufficiently like the English and Russian Revolutions to make it worth our while for some purposes— including those of a science of revolutions—to ignore the differences between them and concentrate upon the similarities by virtue of which we call them all revolutions. Nevertheless, we know very well that they differ in significant ways, and in calling them all revolutions we do not intend to preclude this possibility. It is my contention that the historian, when he sets out to explain the French Revolution is just *not interested* in explaining it as *a* revolution—as an astronomer might be interested in explaining a certain eclipse as an instance of eclipses; he is almost invariably concerned with it as *different* from other members of its class. Indeed, he might even say that his main concern will be to explain the French Revolution's taking a course unlike any other; that is to say, he will explain it as unique in the sense distinguished above. As long as the historian sticks to the problem he has set himself, he cannot appeal to a covering generalization derived from general knowledge of revolutions. For the most such a law could do is explain the French Revolution *qua revolution*, whereas the historian will almost certainly want to take its peculiarities into account as well.

Hempel emphasizes the fact that *neither* science nor history can "grasp the unique individuality of its object", and he reminds us that in *both* of these fields investigators neverthe-less classify what they explain. But to leave it at that fails to bring out important differences in the way scientists and historians commonly use their classification words. For once a scientist can say that what he is going to explain is 'a so-and-so', he is in a position to bring it under law—to explain it as an instance or a case. But when an historian calls his object of study 'a so-and-so', whether his classificatory term is drawn from a social science or from ordinary language, his problem situation is quite different. Indeed, it would only be a slight exaggeration to say that the historian is *never* content to explain what he studies at the level of generality indicated by his classificatory word. A complex classificatory term like 'French Revolution' only *indicates* what is to be explained while its analysis by the historian proceeds. The linguistic machinery by which he manages to maintain this janus-faced attitude toward his object of study is his use of the definite article. Of course the scientist also uses the definite article. But there is no logical parallel between, for example, the naturalist's expression 'the whale', or the economist's 'the business cycle', and the historian's 'the French Revolution'. In economic science, when an explanation of the business cycle is projected, it is assumed that aspects of the cycle entering into the explanation will be recurring ones only. The assumption in the historical case would be quite the contrary.

It is thus misleading to say without qualification that the historian's use of classificatory words supports the thesis that if historical events are to be explicable they must be recurring phenomena.[1] For although it is true that, since historical

---

[1] That history is concerned with recurring phenomena or routines has also, of course, been denied on other grounds. E. H. Carr, in *The New Society*

events can be classified, they are recurring phenomena in the sense that a number of them can be described by means of a single classificatory term, to admit this is not to admit that the explanation of any of them *depends* on their being classified at a level which represents them as recurring phenomena falling under some law. And, as I have shown, this is just what covering law theorists often either say or imply.

It is important to distinguish my argument here from Gardiner's contention that historical terms, e.g. 'revolution', because they are drawn from ordinary language rather than from the precise terminology of a formal science, are likely to be vague, and hence open to further analysis. For even if such a term *were* vague, it would not be *because* of this that an historian would take account of the peculiarities of anything he classified under it—peculiarities which would find no mention in the definition of the term. For in using *any* descriptive term, the historian would ordinarily consider himself bound to take account of features of an actual case other than those which warranted the classificatory judgement.

I should like to make it clear, too, that I am not, in this connexion, claiming that the *complexity* of the historian's subject-matter raises practical difficulties for explanation on the covering law model. Such complexity does, no doubt, create a presumption that it will be difficult to recognize recurrences in history. But an object of study can be complex without being unique—as is the case, for instance, in some of the organic sciences. That the French Revolution is complex does not prevent its being explained as typical; it does not prevent its being regarded as an 'instance' of a law of revolutions. What prevents this is what Oakeshott calls a *presupposition* of historical inquiry. As Oakeshott puts it, to treat the French Revolution as an instance of anything is to abandon historical inquiry for scientific. "The moment historical facts

(London, 1951), observes: "In history the presumption is not that the same thing will happen again but that the same thing will not happen again" (p. 6); but his reason for saying this is that human beings, having both free will and some knowledge of what happened before, deliberately *avoid* repeating the actions of their predecessors.

are regarded as instances of general laws", he maintains, "history is dismissed."[1] Properly understood, this dictum appears to me to be both true and important; for what it brings to our attention is the *characteristic* approach of historians to their subject-matter.

6. *The Role of Historical Judgement*

I have argued that even though a particular explanation has a covert universality about it, this universality is not such as to warrant our accepting covering law theory as it is usually presented. And I have tried to show the sense in which the historian's explanation may be given of, and in terms of, events and conditions which are unique.

But covering law theorists will probably feel that their main contention has still not been given proper consideration. Our examination of the covering law claim has, it is true, shown that the historian can *assert* a particular explanation without committing himself to a covering law of any methodological interest; but what of the further question of how he can *defend* what he thus asserts? The argument from meaning may have failed to show that the historian's explanation 'requires' a covering empirical law in any sense with important practical consequences; but what of the *argument from challenge* which was mentioned and put aside at an earlier stage of the discussion? If the historian wished to convince a sceptic that it was really because of what he mentions in his explanation that the event under examination took place, would he not have to produce evidence for believing that *whenever* such conditions occur, events of this sort result? And if he could not, would he not have to admit that his original explanation, if not 'pseudo', was at any rate dogmatic? In our discussion so far, the onus of proof has been placed upon the logician. But should we not have placed it the other way around?

Like most covering law theorists, Gardiner maintains that a particular explanatory statement must, or must ultimately, be

[1] *Experience and Its Modes*, p. 154.

defended by referring to "the generalization which warrants its utterance". Yet, as he goes on candidly to admit, an historian would seldom *in practice* set about defending his explanation in this way. Indeed, he seems to me to gauge the historian's reaction to challenge quite correctly when he says that he would regard what he explains as "the outcome of a particular complex of factors". If it was the explanation of Louis XIV's unpopularity in terms of his policies that was in question, the historian would therefore defend his original conclusion by filling in further details of the particular situation under review. Indeed, if pressed, he might bring in as 'supporting considerations' all those positive and negative conditions which, in our discussion of the argument from meaning, we imagined the logician adding to the historian's explanation in order to 'complete' it. No doubt a point might be reached at which it was no longer worth making reference to further features of the situation; and at that point the argument would rest. But at this, and every other, stage of his defence, the historian's appeal would be, not to a covering law, but to his opponent's *judgement* that unpopularity would result from such a set of conditions. As Trevelyan puts it, in the course of an explanatory account of the years preceding the English Civil War, the historian's problem is to "*weigh* the prospects of revolt".[1]

That judgement of particular cases, without knowledge of covering laws, actually takes place in history, perhaps few exponents of the model would want to deny. The doctrine of implicit law is really an attempt to convince historians that such judgement ought to be replaced, or be replaceable under fire, by deduction from empirically validated laws. What the exponent of the model will be reluctant to allow is that any defence of the historian's explanation short of appeal to a covering law could really certify it as fully warranted—as rationally acceptable. Yet in view of the fact that when the

---

[1] *The English Revolution*, London, 1938, p. 93. My italics. (It should be clear that I do not employ the term 'judgement' here in the technical sense developed by idealist logicians.)

historian's explanation specifies events or states of affairs which are unique it would be *pointless* to look for a covering empirical generalization, the alternative would seem to be to maintain that in such cases the historian falls *incorrigibly* into 'pseudo' explanation. And this conclusion would be no more welcome to those who wish to make history more 'scientific'.

Perhaps covering law theorists will insist that, once again, the apparent difficulty arises out of a too crude interpretation of the model's claims. For although it is natural to assume, from a great deal of what covering law theorists say, that, if an explanation is to stand scrutiny, a *single* law must be found to cover it, it is sometimes said only that the explicandum must be shown to be logically deducible from the explicans. And it is conceivable that this condition could be satisfied by citing, not one covering law, but a *number* of non-covering ones. Indeed, covering law theorists have sometimes explicitly stated their claims in terms of a plurality of laws. Thus Hempel distinguishes genuine from pseudo explanation by its "use of universal empirical hypotheses"; and Gardiner, at one point, observes that "it is usually the case that not one, but many, generalizations . . . must be used to guide the historian in his quest".[1] Would the formulation of the model in terms of such a plurality of laws undermine the argument which has so far been developed against its simpler, more popular forms?

If the more complicated version of the model is to convey the full covering law thesis, the set of realistic but non-covering laws must, of course, perform the same logical function as the unrealistic but covering one: they must make inference from the conditions designated as complete explanation logically tight. There are two ways in which it might be thought possible to satisfy this condition. One of them is suggested by the following analysis by Hempel of an explanation of a familiar physical event:

Let the event to be explained consist in the cracking of an automobile radiator during a cold night. The sentences of group (1) may state the following initial and boundary conditions: The car was left in the

[1] Op. cit., pp. 98–99.

street all night. Its radiator, which consists of iron, was completely filled with water, and the lid was screwed on tightly. The temperature during the night dropped from 39° F. in the evening to 25° F. in the morning; the air pressure was normal. The bursting pressure of the radiator material is so and so much.—Group (2) would contain empirical laws such as the following: Below 32° F., under normal atmospheric pressure, water freezes. Below 39·2° F., the pressure of a mass of water increases with decreasing temperature, if the volume remains constant or decreases; when the water freezes, the pressure again increases. Finally, this group would have to include a quantitative law concerning the change of pressure of water as a function of its temperature and volume.

From statements of these two kinds, the conclusion that the radiator cracked during the night can be deduced by logical reasoning; an explanation of the considered event has been established.[1]

Such an explanation does not consist of subsumption of the event under a 'law of cracking radiators'; it consists first of an analysis of the gross event into a number of components, and the deduction stepwise of the final result from statements of initial conditions and a number of general laws. The historical parallel in, say, the explanation of the French Revolution would presumably involve, first, an analysis of the event into components like the meeting of the States General, the swearing of the Tennis Court Oath, the trial of the king, &c., and also, perhaps, 'components' which are not themselves events, e.g. the nationalist fervour of the new republic, the cleavage between middle class assemblymen and the Parisian proletariat—in short, whatever the historian feels obliged to mention in his description of what is to be explained. The second step would be the accounting for each component in the original covering law way. When the components were all law-covered, then the Revolution would be rendered predictable—not as a whole, but piecemeal; and it would, at the same time, be fully explained.

That such a piecemeal approach is closer to the historian's usual procedure than a holistic one is unquestionably true; and the revised presentation of the covering law claim is therefore an improvement. It cuts out the suggestion of having to hunt

[1] Op. cit., p. 460.

for parallels, at any rate at the gross level—the level indicated by the historian's classificatory term 'revolution'. But recognizing the complexity—even the uniqueness—of the explained event in this way does not, in itself, render the claim of the covering law theorist acceptable. For the problem of uniqueness may recur for every attempt to subsume a component event (or aspect, or feature) of the gross event under law. In connexion with the independent subsumption of each of these there may develop a dialectic between logician and historian of the kind which we have already examined. It is, of course, always possible that *some* of the details analysed out for explanation may be recognized as routines, and thus as falling under a law. But it is surely unplausible to say that all must be; and it is simply false to say that, in typical historical cases, all in fact will be.

The uniqueness of the historian's explicans thus presents more of a problem for the covering law theorist than the uniqueness of his explicandum. For to a large extent, the uniqueness of what is to be explained is a matter for decision; it is traceable to the historian's interests, his 'approach' to his subject matter, his 'presuppositions'. But the uniqueness of what is offered as explanation is something which the historian discovers—something which he generally cannot ignore.

Yet it may be thought that even this does not present insuperable difficulties for the covering law claim in its more complex version. For there is another way in which a plurality of laws, rather than a single one, might be thought to perform the covering function—a way suggested by Gardiner's remark that "historians offer several causes for an event of any degree of magnitude or complexity".[1] This remark follows a warning that "it is rarely true that [the historian] reached his conclusion by presupposing one simple law. . ."; and the suggestion would appear to be that in explaining an event like the French Revolution, or a state of affairs like the unpopularity of Louis XIV, a general law will be 'appealed to' in the citing of each of a number of explanatory conditions (Gardiner calls them

[1] Op. cit., p. 98.

'causes') *as* a condition. The contention presumably is that the only reason there could be for saying that something *is* a condition is knowledge of a law linking events of that type with events like the one to be explained, although *ex hypothesi* what is explained cannot be deduced from any single condition and law. The covering law claim would now be, however, that a satisfactory explanation would have to specify conditions and laws such that from the *conjunction* of statements listing both conditions and laws the occurrence of what is explained could be deduced.

What does such an account leave out? The missing element is surely a 'law' or 'rule' which would inform the historian when such a group of 'predisposing' conditions becomes sufficient. Laws which allow him to regard each of a number of conditions as 'favouring' the occurrence of what is to be explained cannot simply be assumed to constitute a covering conjunction allowing the explicandum to be deduced from the explicans. No doubt they may, in some cases, allow the conclusion that the revolution or unpopularity could reasonably have been predicted. But such a conclusion would be reached by an exercise of the historian's judgement in the particular case, of the kind we have already considered. Collating a number of conditions, including supporting laws, is not applying a further *covering* law, perhaps in a vague way. It is doing something quite different and much more difficult.[1]

It is worth emphasizing, in this connexion, that the distinction between concluding that something was *certain* to happen, and concluding that it was only *probable* does not coincide with the distinction between *deducing* in accordance with a covering law (or laws) and *judging* in the light of supporting laws. The historian might judge, for instance, that the English Civil War was inevitable in the light of the particular conditions and general considerations mentioned in explaining it—although no covering law or covering conjunction of

---

[1] This would appear to be the kind of problem Mandelbaum has in mind when he contrasts subsumption under law with 'a full causal explanation'. His point is misunderstood and attacked by Gardiner (op. cit., p. 84) and Hempel (op. cit., p. 461, n. 1).

laws could be appealed to. On the other hand, he might deduce, from a covering 'probability hypothesis', that a civil war was only probable in 1641. If this distinction is recognized, logicians may be less likely to insist, in support of the doctrine of implicit law, that although plausible *universal* laws cannot be extracted out of typical explanatory statements in history, the latter may nevertheless be thought of as applying *non*-universal laws. For in cases where the historian concludes that what happened was only probable, if he used laws at all, his argument would be of the form: 'In the light of $C_1 \ldots C_n$, and if C_1 then E_1 (&c.), probably E.' It is an evasion of the historian's usual problem to schematize it as: 'In the light of C, and if C then probably E, probably E.'

The only explanation I can offer of covering law theorists' failure to take seriously the peculiarities of the historian's typical problem—the weighing of a set of miscellaneous 'factors', which cannot be reduced to deduction from general laws—is a certain guiding prejudice: a desire to represent reasoning of all kinds in simple, formal terms. This prejudice displays itself in an interesting way in Gardiner's discussion of the way a practical man, a general, decides what line of action to adopt—a discussion which may appear to accord with the argument of the present chapter, but from which covering law conclusions are nevertheless drawn.[1]

"Generals", Gardiner observes, "appreciate a situation before initiating a policy"; a particular decision is said to be justified if reasons can be produced which "considered together and *ceteris paribus* strongly *suggest* or *support* the conclusion that the course of action ... will be successful. ..". We should not expect that such reasons will exhibit "the elements of the situation as values of precisely formulated invariant laws"—for this would be a "misunderstanding of the logic of practical choice". And "the historian, like the general or statesman, tends to *assess* rather than to *conclude*". "A postulated historical explanation is not, as a rule, justified (or challenged) by demonstrating that a given law implied by

[1] Op. cit., pp. 94-95.

it does (or does not) hold; far less by showing such a law to follow (or not to follow) from an accepted theory or hypothesis, or to be confirmed (or falsified) by experiment; nor again by pointing out that the case under consideration does (or does not) satisfy in the required respects the conditions exactly specified in the formulation of the law."

How then *is* it justified? This question, in spite of what has been said about the parallel from military decision, drives Gardiner to the conclusion that the factors included in the historian's explanation must "be seen to satisfy the antecedent of a general hypothetical"; for unless they do so, "how then is the force of the 'because' to be accounted for . . . ?"[1] The Humean assumption that nothing but 'regularity' can justify a 'because' is thus made from the beginning, and it is too strong to be shaken by information about the way historical arguments actually go. Gardiner does introduce the notion of 'judgement'; but he cannot bring himself entirely to abandon the view that judgement of a particular case is disreputable without the logical *support* of covering empirical laws —laws which 'warrant' the explanation. If the historian does not use a precise 'rule', then a vague one *must* be found; if no universal law is available, then a qualified one *must* have been assumed. The alternative which is too much to accept is that, in any ordinary sense of the word, the historian may use *no law at all.*

[1] Op. cit., pp. 97–98.

EXPLAINING AND PREDICTING

1. *Covering Law as a Sufficient Condition*

IN the preceding chapter I have tried to show that although there may be a grain of truth in the claim that being able to indicate a covering law is a *necessary* condition of giving an explanation, the claim as it is usually made is both logically artificial and methodologically misleading. It obscures distinctions of logical and methodological interest by failing to recognize the extent to which words like 'use', 'function', 'implicit', 'requires', 'law', &c., which commonly appear in its formulation, are susceptible of further analysis, and it fails to take account of the legitimate sense in which historians explain conditions and events which are unique. In the present chapter I want to examine in a similar way the claim that citing a covering law, together with statements setting forth antecedent conditions, is a *sufficient* condition of giving an explanation; and once again, I shall urge that although there is an element of truth in it, this claim, too, is artificial and misleading. In the course of the investigation I shall try to make some progress toward a more satisfactory general account of the logic of 'explanation', by comparing what is offered as explanation in history with what is offered in some other fields.

In asking the question we now have to consider, we approach the problem of what it is to give an explanation from an altogether different direction. The question is no longer whether, in some interesting sense, we *must* have a law, but rather, supposing that we have an appropriate empirical law, whether we then *ipso facto* have the materials for giving an explanation. For in spite of historians' interest in the unique, and although in some cases there is no covering law to which one could sensibly be said to appeal, it would be rash to deny that routines are *ever* recognized in history. Indeed, historians sometimes explicitly point out that the events they study fall under some law or laws. Even Fisher, in spite of his notorious belief that history is 'one great fact', with respect to which there can be no generalization, when explaining the course of Roman expansion, allows himself to remark: "an orderly power ringed about by turbulence always finds itself compelled to establish peace and security upon its frontiers."[1] What I now wish to question is the view that to point to such a generalization is necessarily to explain what falls under it as an instance. I shall argue that something more than this is required, and that to fail to recognize this is to misconceive the logic of 'explanation'.

In putting the problem in this way, I shall be pursuing the kind of inquiry sketched at the beginning. Our question is: 'What are the conditions which have to be met in order to give an explanation in history?' Covering law theorists seem to, and are commonly taken to, say that there is one and only one condition: subsumption under an independently validated general law. Or, as Popper and Hempel both put it: the logical structure of *explanation* is equivalent to that of *prediction* and *verification*, one logical model serving to elucidate what we mean by all three. In the preceding chapter, in the interests of an orderly consideration of various grounds for dissatisfaction with the covering law model, I did not question the view that explanation is just 'prediction upside down'; my argument was rather that neither explanation nor prediction need be law-covered in historical cases. I now want to argue, however, that there is a logical dissimilarity between explanation and prediction of the greatest importance, and that to regard them as strictly correlative operations is to depart from the ordinary meaning of the term 'explanation', which is also its meaning in history. I shall argue that, because of this dissimilarity, it would be incorrect to say that if a person knows that a certain event occurred, and he has information from which it might justifiably have been predicted, then he has all that is needed to explain the event in question.

[1] Quoted by S. Hook, in *The Hero in History*, London, 1945, p. 144.

It is possible that, upon reflection, some of those who support the model's claims would not accept quite such a strict interpretation of what they say. Thus, although Hempel declares that an explanation "is not complete unless it might as well have functioned as a prediction", he does not actually say in so many words that this is the *only* requirement to be met.[1] But, on the other hand, he says nothing to suggest that anything more *is* required—various other criteria being mentioned only to be discarded as the marks of 'pseudo' explanation. And Gardiner, in the course of his exposition of Hume's regularity analysis of causation, tells us that 'an event is explained when it is brought under a generalization or law. It becomes an instance of a general rule. . . .'[2] This account, he adds, is "substantially correct"; and the only qualifications he actually makes are the ones outlined in Chapter I: that in historical contexts we shall find dispositional explanation falling outside this analysis, and that the generalization in other cases will be quite vague because of its loose component terms, its wide *ceteris paribus* clause, &c. I can find nothing in either Gardiner's or Hempel's formulations which would indicate disagreement with the more precise statement of another covering law theorist that "the logical core of explanation is provided by extensional connections or 'subsumptions'. . . . Where we have this pattern, nothing else is needed for explanation; where we lack it, nothing else suffices."[3]

In ' "If", "So" and "Because" ', Ryle puts the same general point in another way. In Ryle's terminology both arguments and explanations are 'applications' of a corresponding hypothetical or inference license. An argument of the form 'p so q' requires the covering hypothetical 'if p then q', in the sense that it is only valid if 'if p then q' is true. Similarly, argues Ryle, 'q because p' also requires 'if p then q', and is an application of it, although in a different way.[4] The latter phrase may seem promising to those who feel uneasy about the covering

<hr>

[1] Op. cit., p. 462.   [2] Op. cit., p. 1.
[3] D. C. Williams, 'Some Remarks on Causation and Compulsion', *Journal of Philosophy*, 1953, p. 123. See also the passage quoted from Hook in Chap. I, section 2.   [4] p. 331.

law claim; but the only difference actually brought out is the fact that although 'p' and 'if p then q' are all that is required to justify the argument 'p so q', it is not the case that 'q' and 'if p then q' are all that is required to justify the explanation 'q because p'—for we also need independent knowledge of 'p'. This difference is, of course, a genuine one. But I shall argue in this chapter that even so, we might still deny that 'p' and 'if p then q' give an explanation of 'q'.

2. *Generalizations and Explanatory Theories*

If covering law theorists were right in claiming that their model formulates a sufficient condition of explaining something, then reference to a covering law ought *always* to explain what falls under its apodosis clause. But it is surely not difficult to think of cases from everyday affairs which furnish evidence to the contrary. When puzzled by something, we do not ordinarily find it enlightening to be told: 'That's what always happens.' Indeed, although such a remark appears to be just an idiomatic, incomplete way of subsuming what happened under a general law, we should often feel justified in protesting: 'That's no explanation at all.'

What, for instance, is the explanatory force of the common-sense generalization, 'Red sky in the morning is followed by rain'? Does the fact that the sky was red this morning *explain* the fact that rain fell before lunch? Surely not. Translated into Ryle's symbolism, what happens in such cases is that although 'p' and 'q' and 'if p then q' are all true, still 'p' does not explain 'q'—which on his account is impossible. The hypothetical licenses the corresponding argument, but it does not license the explanation. Having a good reason for expecting something is not necessarily being able to explain why it occurs. This fact may easily be obscured by a purely formal analysis of the relation between different types of sentence. For it is necessary to distinguish 'because' sentences which only represent 'p' as a *reliable inductive sign* of 'q' from those which represent it as *the explanation* of 'q'. Suppose someone says: 'It will rain before lunch because the sky was red this morning.' Since Ryle's symbolism is tense-neutral, it would be quite proper to render this as 'q because p'. In such a use the relation between the 'because' sentence and the covering hypothetical is exactly what Ryle says it is: nothing more than the hypothetical is required to license the 'because'. But this is because the latter is now just the argument itself in a different form. This conclusion can be supported by noticing the circumstances under which it would be possible to say 'q because p' with the values indicated by the present example. We should say this only when we do not know independently that 'q' is true, and this is exactly the condition under which we argue 'p so q'.

The failure of at any rate some general laws to explain particular cases falling under them is even more obvious if we happen to select a classificatory generalization—for instance, that favourite of the formal logicians, 'All swans are white'. Such a general 'law' might, perhaps, at some stage of its career, achieve the status of an analytic statement. But as long as we did not make 'whiteness' a defining characteristic of swans, and the 'law' thus remained a true generalization, reference to it could scarcely be represented as explaining the fact that any particular swan was white. The most it could conceivably do in an explanatory way is explain why an investigator might say that a swan, as yet unobserved, would be white; that is, it would merely provide his justification for predicting its colour. Why then should a medieval historian who has discovered, say, that Sir Brian Tuke was bow-legged, be expected to regard as explanatory the assurance of a more experienced colleague that all medieval knights were?

Merely knowing that a red morning sky is always followed by rain would not explain today's downpour. Merely knowing that all medieval knights were bow-legged would not explain Sir Brian's bandy knees. In the face of such difficulties, some covering law theorists appear, at times, to be prepared to modify the sufficient condition claim by drawing a distinction between different *kinds* of laws. A distinction of this sort is often made, for instance, between mere empirical generaliza-

tions and the laws of the theoretical sciences. Thus Professor
S. Toulmin, in *The Philosophy of Science*, represents empirical
generalizations, arrived at inductively by the observation of
similar cases, as proper only in that branch of science called
'natural history'—a descriptive rather than explanatory study.[1]
For genuine explanations we are referred to branches of
science using higher level theoretical laws, which cannot be
discovered by simple induction at all—such laws as 'Light
travels in straight lines', or 'Gases have a molecular structure'.
That light travels in straight lines (at least partly) explains the
fact that the shadow thrown by a 10-foot wall at sun's eleva-
tion 45° is 10 feet. That gases have a molecular structure (at
least partly) explains why a balloon of air expands when
heated.

Our concern here is, of course, with explanation in history
rather than what Popper calls the 'pure generalizing sciences'.
But I think it will be worth our while to look briefly at this
distinction which philosophers of science sometimes draw between different kinds of laws. For, although no full analysis
can be attempted, there are certain logical differences between
the two which seem to me suggestive for a general account of
explanation which departs from the covering law model.

What is it about a theoretical law which gives it explanatory
force? The most common answer is that the laws of a theoretical science do not, so to speak, stand on their own; they are
components of explanatory theories, often of very great scope.
Individual laws like the ones mentioned above get their full
meaning only in terms of the theories from which they are
derived—in the case of our examples, the geometrical theory
of optics and the molecular theory of gases. Theory and law
are set up together; they are made for each other. Indeed, it is
scarcely an exaggeration to say that when a law of this sort is
called upon to explain a case falling under it, it is the whole
theory which is brought to bear. The theory is implicitly
called upon in the sense that only if we know the theoretical
background will reference to the law itself explain. As we often

[1] London, 1953, especially chap. iii.

put it, the phenomena are explained *in terms of* the theory (a phrase which, I shall argue later, is suggestive of the explanatory force of theories).

But when the question is pushed a stage farther, and we ask why such indirect reference to whole theories is explanatory while reference to a mere covering generalization is not, we generally find covering law theorists, and even some who would not count themselves as such, reverting to the essentials of the position which we have just questioned, namely that an explanation is satisfactory in so far as the data contained in it could have functioned as a prediction mechanism. Thus we find Toulmin calling theories 'inference techniques', as if it were this characteristic which distinguished them from empirical generalizations arrived at by simple inductive inquiry.[1] (Whether he would say they are *mere* inference techniques, I am not sure.) But an inference technique, or license, could be derived from a generalization *or* a theory; what we have to discover is in what respects the latter differs in explanatory force.

The answer which emphasizes the inference-licensing role of the theory shows that, in spite of the promising distinction made between the two types of general statement, the covering law thesis remains intact. For we are told that the difference between the two is one of scope, generality or power—and it is *predictive* power which is meant. To use Rylian language, theories are many-sided in their applicability; they consist of hypotheticals which are highly determinable, not determinate; open, rather than highly specified. 'All swans are white' applies only to swans and only to them in respect of their whiteness. 'Light travels in straight lines' applies to shadow lengths, telescopic sightings, eclipses, mirror images, and a host of other phenomena. It applies not only to many different cases, but to many different kinds of cases. It is in line with this account that Toulmin sometimes says, not that covering generalizations do not explain their cases at all, but that they afford only 'shallow explanations'. 'This rolls downhill because

[1] Op. cit., p. 28.

it is a stone, and stones generally do roll downhill' is an explanation which takes us no farther than 'childhood dynamics'.[1]

The notion that the explanatory force of generalizations and of theoretical statements differs only in degree is a popular one. Thus Professor H. Feigl, having characterized explanations as "primarily a procedure of inference (just like the closely related prediction)", and having noted the complex structure of scientific theories, observes: "No wonder that the 'Aha-experience' is much stronger for these deductions from theories than from the more simple deductions from empirical laws."[2] By comparison with the latter, theoretical explanations are "high-grade". Gardiner, too, notes that it is 'the systematic character' of a science which allows it to give explanations with precision and force. Of common-sense explanations using empirical generalizations, he remarks: "They do not make a close structural analysis of the phenomena they roughly link together: they are content to notice a certain simple compresence or succession in experience, and that is all. In consequence, the explanations which they provide are of a vague and frequently unreliable kind, admitting of a multitude of exceptions."[3] Gardiner's lengthy discussion of the role of 'scientific theory and conceptual systems' issues in the conclusion that, in spite of there being differences between highly theoretical explanations and appeals to covering generalizations, the differences are not important for an account of the logic of explanation; for the difference is mainly a matter of the degree of confidence we have in each.

Is there nothing further to be said about the explanatory force of scientific theories? If we accept the account so far given, we are left with a mystery to explain. For to say that a theoretical explanation differs from subsumption under an empirical generalization only in the superior predictive reliability of the theory fails even to suggest why reference to at

[1] Op. cit., p. 50.
[2] 'Some Remarks on the Meaning of Scientific Explanation', reprinted in Feigl and Sellars, *Readings in Philosophical Analysis*, p. 512.
[3] Op. cit., p. 16.

least *some* generalizations provides no explanation at all. And it has the additional disadvantage, it seems to me, of condemning the explanations historians ordinarily give as 'low grade'. For there are few historical events which we can hope to explain in terms of theories borrowed from the special sciences, and there is no such thing as a general theory of history—in the sense of 'theory' employed in the formal sciences.

Some philosophers, it is true, look forward to the day when such a general theory will be constructed; and sociologists often seem to aim at repairing the deficiency. Other philosophers and methodologists of history regard the hope of constructing such a theory as illusory in view of the historian's concern with a concrete and miscellaneous subject matter. But whether such an enterprise has any likelihood of success or not, it would surely be unplausible to maintain that the giving of a genuine, or even of a 'high-grade', explanation in history must await the theory's formulation. For historians seem *already* to be able to explain at least some events to their own satisfaction. Perhaps typical explanation in history is not a lower grade version of the scientific kind, but something with logical peculiarities of its own. Perhaps what Feigl calls the 'Aha-experience' does not just arise out of our recognizing the predictive possibilities of the set of theoretical statements sometimes brought into the explanation of a particular state of affairs.

3. The Model of the Continuous Series

Let me attempt to strengthen the case for such a conclusion by discussing in some detail a concrete example from everyday affairs: an example which, in an important way, will be found to lie on middle ground between typical explanations in science, given in terms of a covering theory, and equally typical explanations in history, where no such theories are used. The fact that it is drawn from the sphere of mechanics will make it an especially useful choice for my present purpose, since that will, for the moment, cut out certain complications which are introduced when we consider explanations of

intelligent human actions, complications with which I wish
to deal independently in Chapter V.

Suppose that the engine of my motor-car seizes up, and,
after inspecting it, the garage mechanic says to me: 'It's due
to a leak in the oil reservoir.' Is this an explanation of the
seizure? I should like to argue that it depends on who says it
and to whom—or, to put the matter in more formal terms, it
depends on what else is presupposed, or contextually supplied.
To the assistant mechanic standing near by, who knows all
about internal combustion engines, it may very well be an explanation. To me, who am quite ignorant of what goes on
under the bonnet, it is no explanation at all.

Let us try to put more precisely the difference between
what I have to go on and what the mechanic knows. For I
need not be so uninformed as not to know what is being
referred to by the term 'oil reservoir'. Nor need the mechanic
know 'all about auto engines' in order to transform 'There's
a leak in the oil reservoir' from a mere statement of fact into
an explanation. Would it have been enough, then, if he had
had just enough experience of motor-cars to know that whenever oil reservoirs have leaks, the engine sooner or later seizes
up? This would accord very well with the covering law theory
if it were true; but surely it is not. I could have arrived at such
a generalization by the most careful inductive procedure, and
I might have absolute and justifiable faith in it. There may
never have been a contrary case in the records of this garage,
or of any other one I examine: whenever reservoirs were
leaky, engines may have seized up. But this would make me
none the wiser as to why an oil leak should have led to the
seizure; it does not warrant my claiming that I know 'the
explanation'.

If I am to understand the seizure, I shall need to be told
something about the functioning of an auto engine, and the
essential role in it of the lubricating system. I shall have to be
capable of a certain amount of elementary trouble tracing. I
need to be told, for instance, that what makes the engine go is
the movement of the piston in the cylinder; that if no oil

arrives the piston will not move because the walls are dry;
that the oil is normally brought to the cylinder by a certain
pipe from the pump, and ultimately from the reservoir; that
the leak, being on the underside of the reservoir, allowed the
oil to run out, and that no oil therefore reached the cylinder in
this case. I now know the explanation of the engine stoppage.
What is there in this account that covering law theory leaves
out?

It seems to me that my understanding of the engine seizure
is very directly related to the fact that I can now *trace the course
of events by which it came about*. The mechanism has been
revealed: the oil ran out the hole; nothing came into the
cylinder to lubricate the piston; the movement of the dry
piston against the walls of the cylinder made them hot; the
hot metals expanded and locked tightly. *Of course* the engine
seized up—and I say this because I can now envisage a *continuous series of happenings* between the leak and the engine
seizure which themselves are quite understandable—as the
original sequence 'leak-to-seizure' was not.

Let me make my point clearer by anticipating two likely
objections. The first, which is a version of the argument used
by Russell in his well-known essay on causation,[1] is that the
idea of a 'continuous series' is philosophically naïve because
of the infinite divisibility of space and time. Russell used this
argument to outlaw the word 'cause' from science, but this
aspect of it need not concern us here.

It does not seem to me that such an argument from spatio-
temporal infinity raises any real difficulty for the point I wish
to make. For there is no harm in admitting that the various
sub-events which would have to be mentioned in an explanatory account of the engine seizure form a continuous series in
a relative rather than an absolute sense. That is not to say
merely that each link in the chain of circumstance is itself
closer to some ideal of continuity, so that the best explanation
would be the one which carried the process farthest. The
point is rather that in offering a sum of sub-sequences to

---

[1] 'On the Notion of Cause', in *Mysticism and Logic*, London, 1918.

explain a gross one, the former must be *acceptable* to some
person, investigator, craft, audience, &c. They must themselves raise no further demand for explanation in that particular context. They are—to use a convenient term of Dr. F.
Waismann's—'hat-doffing' phenomena.[1] They do not puzzle
us; we ask no questions of them; we just 'take off our hats to
them'. So although Russell's objection to the notion of a continuous series is, in a sense, formally sound, it is pragmatically
false. And, as I shall argue further in this, and succeeding,
chapters, there is an irreducible pragmatic dimension to explanation. In a case like the one under consideration, it would,
of course, be open to anyone to question whether a particular
series is, in fact, a continuous one. But this, although it may
reveal what is a 'hat-doffing' phenomenon for him, does not
prove that no series are ever continuous, i.e. that the term
'continuous series' has no use.

The second objection may seem at first a more embarrassing
one. For a covering law theorist might at this point ask how
my admittedly more complicated account of what is required
to explain the engine seizure differed in any *logical* way from
the covering law theory itself. For what I call 'hat-doffing'
sub-sequences, it may be contended, are surely themselves
accepted and unquestioned just because they are 'what always
happens', 'what was to have been expected under the circumstances'; and since, in the present chapter, the claims of the
model on its necessary condition side are not being questioned,
these sub-sequences can be regarded as straightforward cases
of subsumption under law. No doubt we often find it desirable
to break down a big explanatory job into parts, each to be
dealt with separately; and the way this is sometimes done in
history has already been discussed.[2] But the question to be
answered here is whether, in cases where although we do not
just call upon a single covering law, we nevertheless call upon
a covering conjunction of them, any other logical criterion is
applied. And the covering law objector will regard it as obvious
that it is not.

---

[1] See Toulmin, op. cit., p. 117.   [2] In Chap. II, section 6.

The objection is both plausible and important. But I want to insist that what is added to covering law requirements by the analysis of our example is essential, and that it is a logical condition of giving the explanation—at any rate, in the broad sense of 'logic' familiar among analytic philosophers. For it is my claim that it is essential to the notion of giving an explanation that even if subsumption under law were a necessary condition of it, there should be criteria which allow us to distinguish some law-covered phenomena from others.

The difference between my analysis of the present example and that of the standard covering law theory could be emphasized thus. The general law, 'Whenever your oil leaks out your engine seizes up', does not explain the fact that my engine seized up after my oil leaked out—in the context of puzzlement envisaged. But reference to a series of facts constituting the story of what happened between the leakage of the oil and the seizure of the engine does explain the seizure. Even if it were true that these smaller scale events were each covered by law in the sense that in every case I would be prepared to assent to a law corresponding to a sub-sequence, the laws involved would be, at most, part of the explanation of the gross event, not of the sub-event they cover; so that when they do function in an explanation they are not *covering* laws at all.

Thus, although the engine seizure—the gross event—may be said to be explained by assuming many sub-laws like, 'When the walls of a cylinder and piston are dry they heat and expand with motion', the law mentioned would not in turn explain why the piston expands and heats up—if we were to go on to ask that question. The sub-law is part of the explanation of the gross event, although it does not *cover* it; the same law covers the sub-event, although it does not *explain* it. Once a gross event has been seen to require an explanation, then there is a two-levelled structure of events and laws to be reckoned with. Satisfactory explanation, if it employs laws at all, employs laws only of the lower level. To appeal to a gross covering law would be, in effect, to short-circuit the real work the explanation is intended to do. Subsumption under such a law can scarcely, therefore, be represented as a sufficient condition of giving the explanation.

Let me try to clarify my point by anticipating a further difficulty which may seem to lurk behind the claim I am making. I have said that a gross law does not explain the gross event; for this we need sub-laws. And I might have added that the sub-laws, in turn, do not explain the sub-events; for this we need sub-sub-laws, and so on. The conclusion which may falsely be drawn from this is that nothing can ever really be explained, for the attempt to give an explanation leads us directly into an infinite regress. For some philosophers the explanatory regress has seemed to go in another, but equally embarrassing direction. Thus McTaggart, having denied that merely subsuming an event under a law explains it, intimates that this is because "the law itself has not been explained". And no matter how far you carry a hierarchy of higher-order laws explaining lower-order ones, you eventually have to accept a "law which is ultimate and cannot be explained further".[1]

This very common pattern of argument is quite illegitimate —at any rate as a proof that we can never explain anything, or even that we can never explain anything *satisfactorily*. As I was careful to say, the law covering the piston's behaviour does not explain why it heats up *if we should go on to ask that question*. The condition italicized should be taken seriously; for this is *not* the question which was answered appropriately in terms of laws at the level of the piston's behaviour. Should we decide to *change* our question to 'Why did the piston heat up?', then it would become necessary to go beyond laws of the sub-level, and so on. No doubt if we adopt the policy of *continually* changing our question, it will be impossible for anyone to produce an answer which we shall be prepared to accept as a satisfactory explanation. But so long as we ask one question at a time, no regress occurs.

---

[1] *Philosophical Studies*, London, 1934, p. 166. McTaggart puts the point in terms of *causal* laws, but I suppress the qualifying term to avoid needless complication here. But see Chapter IV.

To put it another way: a person who adopts the *policy* of always refusing to accept an *x* as the explanation of *y* unless the *x* is itself explained, begins to empty the term 'explanation' of its normal meaning. And if he goes on—as I suspect many objectors do without realizing it—to demand that any explanation of a *y* in terms of an *x* should *at the same time* explain *x* (and so on, *ad infinitum*), he empties the term of all meaning. He really no longer knows what he means when he asks for an explanation; he does not know what would count as one. But we need not take even the first step toward such a position, for a complete or satisfactory explanation is not necessarily one given in terms of what is itself explained. It is in terms rather of what (for the moment, or at this level, or for the purpose of this inquiry, &c.) does not require explanation. It is part of the *logic* of 'explanation' that if something can be explained, there is something else which does not require explanation. But the reason it does not require explanation is not necessarily that we know its explanation already.

4. *The Ordinary Meaning of 'Explain'*

The example of the engine seizure might be regarded as setting up, against covering law theory, a 'model of the continuous series'. Such a model does not necessarily apply to everything which is legitimately called 'explanation'; nor do I wish to suggest that the discussion of the preceding section brings out all the important features of those explanations to which it does apply. But it does, at any rate, provide a useful corrective to the covering law model as it is usually elaborated. It brings out, for instance, the force of saying, as some philosophers do, that explanation is concerned with finding 'middle terms'.[1]

It would appear, indeed, that there is an *essential* complexity about what is ordinarily considered explanatory; that once the demand for explanation arises, an answer which does no more than represent what is to be explained as what we always find happening in such circumstances fails to explain it at all. The

[1] e.g. M. R. Cohen, 'Causation and its Application to History', *Journal of the History of Ideas*, 1942, p. 18.

complexity, the element of *analysis* of the case under consideration, need not always take the form displayed by the engine seizure—it may not, for instance, be a temporal account. But some sort of analysis besides mere certification as a recurring phenomenon, would seem to be essential. I assume, of course, that the demand for explanation arises out of a genuine puzzlement, and that the explanation is offered in good faith—not as a joke, or in order to silence the questioner. Thus, if the objection were raised that it is common practice for harassed parents to respond to their children's 'why' questions with 'That's what always happens', I should insist that such a response, far from being an explanation, is just a way of registering either their inability or their unwillingness to give one.

I should like to make it clear that the application of the present logical doctrine to historical cases requires more than the mere admission—which many covering law theorists are quite prepared to make—that historians, in giving explanations of what they study, normally want to give a fairly detailed account of what happened. For I have argued, not that explanations often *do* go beyond certifying something as 'What always happens', but rather that they *must*. Mr. Gardiner, for instance, would agree that in seeking an explanation of, say, the unpopularity of Louis XIV, an historian would usually feel obliged to do more than cite a covering law which directly generalized his original explanatory statement. But, on his view, this is only because the gross covering law which might be extracted from that statement is too vague, too unreliable as a guide to prediction, so that it needs to be replaced by one more precisely stated; and it is in order to fill out the antecedent clause of such a law that the historian insists on a close analysis of the particular case. My point is rather that it is the *unintelligibility* of the gross sequence, not just the predictive unreliability of a general law corresponding to it, which makes necessary such further analysis. It is a *pragmatic*, not an inductive, modification of the model's account which is required in this connexion.

Exponents of the model who object to my insisting that we take into account a pragmatic dimension of the concept, may perhaps argue that my belief that this is necessary is traceable to a mistake about the lessons to be drawn from the example of the engine seizure. For it may be alleged that my discussion has failed to draw an important distinction between giving 'the explanation' of something, and giving what amounts to 'an explanation for so-and-so'. It may be said that what I represent as pragmatic criteria of explanation are really not criteria which must be satisfied for something to be an explanation at all; they merely reflect the fact that various individuals find some explanations more satisfactory than others—although all may be formally sound, and all properly called 'explanations'. As Mr. J. Cohen puts it: "What is an explanation for one person may be none at all for another, since its achievement in this direction will vary in accordance with the factual beliefs (or even the emotional make-up and current feelings) of those interested."[1] But in discussing the logic of the concept, Cohen thinks it proper to ignore this 'psychological category of explanation'. And what is left turns out to be analysable simply in terms of regularity.

The distinction between giving 'an explanation for so-and-so' and giving 'the explanation' is one which should, I agree, be drawn. But I cannot see that drawing it need be regarded as reinstating the covering law claim. For although the use of the latter expression appears to presuppose objective criteria for what shall count as explanation, while the use of the former presupposes the contrary, the distinction between objectively and subjectively acceptable explanations need not coincide with the distinction between those which are formally and pragmatically sound. There are undoubtedly contexts in which the combination of knowledge and ignorance which gives rise to the demand for explanation, and the standards of intelligibility which will be applied to what is offered as explanation, will vary considerably from person to person. In

[1] 'Teleological Explanation', *Proceedings of the Aristotelian Society*, 1950–1, p. 259.

such contexts there will be no point in speaking of *the* explanation at all. The use of this expression presupposes *shared* criteria, but still criteria of the pragmatic sort. It is not necessary to retreat into a formal definition of 'explanation' as 'showing something to be deducible from a general law' in order to envisage objective standards for what shall count as explanation, although the belief that it *is* necessary may account for some of the reluctance of covering law theorists to regard what I have called the pragmatic dimension of the concept as anything more than a psychological peculiarity.

My claim that we cannot give a proper account of explanation without bringing out its pragmatic dimension obviously harks back to some older-fashioned discussions of the subject. Professor S. Stebbing, for instance, in her *Modern Introduction to Logic*, represents explanation as the reduction of the unfamiliar to the familiar, the unknown to the known. She writes: "What is familiar is usually taken to be understood, so that in its simplest form the answer to the question consists in pointing out a connection between the fact to be explained and something that is familiar."[1] In his *Probability and Induction*, Mr. W. Kneale gives a different account. "An explanation", he says, "must in some sense *simplify* what we have to accept."[2] He thus regards the explanatory use of theoretical laws (he calls them 'transcendent hypotheses') in science as aimed at reducing "the number of transparent necessitations we need to assume". As my discussion of the explanation of human action in Chapter V will show, I do not think that either Stebbing's or Kneale's account, or, indeed both taken together, bring out *all* the non-inductive requirements we recognize in giving explanations. But there is little doubt that both mention important demands which are in fact often made; and that these are appropriately called 'pragmatic'.

Taking account of the pragmatic dimension of explanation brings the analysis of the concept more into line with the way the word is used in the ordinary course of affairs. Besides 'to make clear the cause, origin or reason of', the *Oxford English*

---

[1] 2nd edn., London, 1933, p. 389.   [2] Oxford, 1949, p. 91.

Dictionary gives the following as general meanings of 'explain': 'to smooth out', 'to unfold', 'to give details of', 'to make plain or intelligible', 'to clear of obscurity or difficulty'.[1] The model of the continuous series, with its suggestion of unrolling or revealing what was previously unknown or puzzling, is also closer to such common ways of talking as 'explaining my purpose', 'explaining my point of view', 'explaining my meaning', 'explaining the use of this word, that tool, &c.'—all difficult to account for on the covering law model. Such a sampling of ordinary uses of the term 'explain' must at least suggest that the analysis which this model offers cannot have a very wide application—even that it may be a special sense invented for a special purpose.

There is, in fact, some reason for thinking that what the covering law theory gives us is the criterion of a technical sense of 'explanation' found only in narrowly scientific discourse, perhaps only among certain philosophers of science. I remarked in Chapter I that the theory found most of its early support among philosophers who regarded their task as chiefly the analysis of the language and procedures of science, especially physical science. Hempel's formulation begins by laying down the logical structure of explanation as he believes he finds it in physics; he then goes on to show that historical cases approximate to this ideal in varying degrees. There is no apology for the direction of the analysis from physics, where the logical outline is boldly displayed, to other fields, where traces of the model have to be found by dint of careful reconstruction.

Whether a sense of 'explain' is widely employed among theoretical scientists which means no more than 'bring under a general law' I cannot claim to know, although I suspect that it is at any rate less widespread than the philosophers in question would lead us to believe. Professor P. W. Bridgman, for instance, in *The Logic of Modern Physics*, declares that

[1] Explanation in terms of causes is discussed in Chapter IV; explanation in terms of reasons in Chapter V; explanation in the sense of removing difficulty in Chapter VI.

"the essence of an explanation consists in reducing a situation
to elements with which we are so familiar that we accept them
as a matter of course, so that our curiosity rests"[1]—and it is
scientific explanation which he has especially in mind. A
view similar to those expressed by Stebbing and Kneale can
also be found in N. R. Campbell's *Physics, The Elements*.
"Explanation", he writes, "consists in the substitution of
more for less satisfactory ideas. Ideas may be more satisfactory either because they are more familiar or because
they are simpler."[2] Then, directing his attention to scientific
explanation, he continues: "Such explanation of laws as is
effected by other laws is explanation of the second kind, the
explaining ideas being simpler because they are more general."

But it really does not matter for my own argument whether
the majority of scientists and philosophers of science recognize
in the covering law model what *they* commonly mean by
'explanation' when they are doing or describing physics. For
my present aim is to break down the plausibility of the claim
that this restricted meaning—whether it has a legitimate use
elsewhere or not—*must* apply to historical cases, and in this
connexion it is relevant to show that it in fact departs from
the *ordinary* meaning of the term. Furthermore, since the
narrow meaning, as the quotation from Campbell suggests,
is not entirely unrelated to the ordinary one, the former might
be regarded as an abstraction from the latter. For in claiming
that the pragmatic criteria are essential, I have not intended to
deny that the elaboration of a continuous series may often
satisfy the condition that what is explained be predictable
from the data which the explanation contains.

It seems to me that what covering law theorists have done
is to seize on (and, as shown in Chapter II, to misinterpret) a
necessary condition of (some kinds of) explanation which is so
closely connected to the purpose of science—control—that it
has been mistaken for a sufficient condition. 'Explanation', as
covering law theorists use it, is a technical term; and, as such
terms so often do, it abstracts from a term in ordinary use the

---

[1] New York, 1948, p. 37.   [2] Cambridge, 1920, p. 113.

aspect which is of most interest in the kind of inquiry for which it is redesigned. Provided we realize what we are doing, there is no harm in such redefinition of terms. But if scientists, for their own legitimate purposes, redefine 'explain' so that it means roughly what covering law theorists say it does, then we are quite justified in advertising our awareness of what has been done by saying that, in fact, scientists do not seem to be much interested in explanation; they care only for 'explanation' (as technically defined). If the purpose of science is indeed the elaboration of predictive mechanisms rather than (as is still sometimes believed) an attempt to 'understand the world', then the technical term 'explain' will be very useful; it will allow us to indicate in a convenient way phenomena the form of which has been captured by some scientific law or theory. What the philosopher of history must resist is any attempt to force the new concept into currency in situations where the job is to *explain* rather than merely to 'explain'. And this, we may with some justification suspect covering law theorists of having done.

It is all too easy to confuse two questions: the purpose of science and the meaning of explanation. If we keep them distinct, we shall know what to say if a covering law theorist retorts: 'I admit that there is an ordinary meaning of the term "explanation" more or less as you have outlined it, but I am interested only in scientific explanation, and in historical explanation in so far as it is scientific.' Provided that 'scientific' is not simply taken to be equivalent to 'reputable', the proper reply is to invite the objector to show that the technical, derivative sense of 'explanation' is in fact used in history; and if it is not, to show good reason why it should be adopted. That the need for making such a case for it should have been overlooked is due to the too facile assumption of many covering law theorists that common sense and historical explanations are just woollier versions of the kind scientists give, in conjunction with the belief that in science explanation is always given on the covering law model. But once it is suspected that covering law theory, at most, formulates a criterion for a technical sense of the term, a great deal of the persuasiveness of those who urge the adoption of the model as 'scientific' disappears.

5. *Theoretical and Historical Explanation*

I have argued that what covering law theorists really advocate is the importation into historical studies of a special, technical sense of the term 'explanation' designed for narrow scientific uses. But even to say this may not bring out the full extent to which covering law theory *prescribes* a sense of the term, rather than calls attention to one already accepted. For although, as I have already said, it is not my purpose here to assess the adequacy of the covering law model in scientific contexts, it would appear to be at least arguable that reference to a scientific theory may be explanatory in the *ordinary* sense, while reference to a generalization is not. In so far as reference to a theory does give an explanation—in science or elsewhere—it seems to me that it does so not for the quasi-inductive reasons suggested by Gardiner and others, but because it is a means of satisfying just the kind of pragmatic demands which we have been discussing.

How did we come to think that reference to a theory *ipso facto* explained what fell under it? Let me hazard a hypothesis. Why does the theory of geometrical optics explain the length of particular shadows? At the risk of stretching Toulmin's account, it is surely because a ray diagram goes along with it, allowing us to think of light as travelling along ray lines, some of the lines passing over the wall and others coming to a dead halt on its surface. The shadow length is explained when (to use a phrase of Toulmin's) we think of light as 'something travelling', i.e. when we apply to it a very familiar and perhaps anthropomorphic way of thinking. If we were just given an equation or even a geometrical figure, this would not be sufficient to explain the shadow lengths, no matter how faultlessly this mechanism allowed us to calculate them.

Although it may be considered reactionary to say so, it seems to me that scientific theories normally have to meet two quite different demands. First, they must increase our pre-dictive power, i.e. have the characteristic of *generality*. Gar-diner's discussion of the role of scientific theories emphasizes only this aspect. Second, they must explain the phenomena, i.e. have *intelligibility*. It is wrong to think that satisfying the first demand automatically satisfies the second—which is what covering law theorists in effect say in so far as they allow theory a special place in explanation. Some theories, we must admit, may be just inferring techniques, since they may lack a model. But if there are any such, perhaps we should think twice about calling them *explanatory* theories; at most they 'explain', in the technical sense.

My contention is, therefore, that in so far as the light ray theory explains shadow phenomena, it is because of its implicit reference to rays of light running tramlike along celestial rails from a certain source. Similarly, that the volume of a gas expands with increase of heat, is explained by the kinetic theory of gases, in that it allows us to think of gases as com-posed of little particles which increase the momentum with which they strike the sides of their container. Thus the role of theory in such explanations is really *parasitic* upon the fact that it suggests, with the aid of postulated, unobservable entities, a 'hat-doffing' series of happenings which we are licensed to fill in. The theory allows us to tell 'a likely story' behind the appearances. But if the travelling of observable entities along observable rails in a similar way would not explain a similar pattern of impact on encountering a wall, and if the jostling of a tightly packed crowd would not explain the straining and collapsing of the walls of a tent in which they were confined, then the corresponding scientific theories would not explain shadow lengths and the behaviour of gases.

In history, as I have already remarked, explanations are seldom given by means of, or in terms of, theories. In this respect, they are to be contrasted not only with explanations in the formal sciences, but with everyday explanations of the sort illustrated by the engine seizure as well. For the latter was a theoretical explanation of a sort. The mechanic's

announcement, 'There's a leak in the oil reservoir', is explanatory only when taken in conjunction with what we might call
the theory of the internal combustion engine. It is the assistant
mechanic's general knowledge of the way auto engines work
which allows him to fill in for himself the missing links in the
chain of circumstances, on the basis of the chief mechanic's
statement. As in the strictly scientific case, no independent
knowledge of the intervening links of the chain is needed. The
theory itself is sufficient to license the *interpolation* of a 'hat-
doffing' series behind appearances—i.e. under the bonnet.

In another respect, however, the mechanical example is
more like an historical case. For the mechanic's theory licenses
the filling in of potentially observable happenings; the explanation derived from it employs no abstract entities. In typical
historical cases, too, the continuous series constructed by the
historian's explanatory narrative will consist of observable
happenings. The peculiarity of the historical case is that,
normally, each event in the series will be established independently from evidence. There will be no general theory, even
of the mechanical kind, to make detailed research into the
actual course of events unnecessary. But lack of an organizing
theory, as we should now be able to see, need not prevent the
historian from giving explanations which are quite as 'high-
grade' as those given in theoretical terms in other fields. We
often explain by means of, or in terms of, a theory, but there
is nothing in the nature of such explanation which need
persuade us that we cannot explain satisfactorily without one.
For to explain with the aid of a theory is to do indirectly what
the historian, perhaps painstakingly and piecemeal, does
directly: reduce what is puzzling to what is not.

In view of the contrast I have drawn between explanations
in historical and non-historical contexts, it may be of interest,
in concluding this chapter, to turn briefly to Professor White's
question about the nature of specifically historical explanation. For I think that the unsatisfactory answer which he felt
obliged to give to it may now be seen to arise at least partly
out of his prior acceptance of the covering law view of the

logical structure of all explanation. White, it will be remembered, concluded that there were *no* explanations which could properly be called specifically historical. For if all explanation is given by subsumption of case under law, the only way to distinguish *kinds* of explanation, he thinks, is by the use of either laws or terms essential to the various disciplines; and neither principle isolates a class which can plausibly be characterized as 'historical'. Explanations found in history books which do not belong to any of the formal sciences White therefore assigns to the not yet clearly defined social sciences, even though the laws 'presupposed' by them may not have been discovered by certified investigators in these fields, and the terms employed may not at first seem to 'belong' to any particular discipline.

The corollary which White in this way draws from Hempel's statement of the model has not been accepted by all covering law theorists. Professor E. W. Strong, for instance, objects to the suggestion that historians have, from time to time, presupposed non-existing sciences.[1] Herodotus, he allows, used terms which have now been appropriated by psychologists; but this is not to say that he therefore used specifically psychological terms. Gardiner, too, criticizes White's argument on the ground that history is written in ordinary rather than technical language. "A bona fide historical explanation" of the establishment of new hospitals in England after 1700, for instance, would take the form: "they were the outcome of individual initiative and co-ordinated voluntary effort and subscription";[2] and there are no terms in it which are in any way technical. But neither Gardiner nor Strong says what it is about such explanations which make them specifically historical. Gardiner's constant emphasis on the 'looseness' of historical language may, indeed, give the impression that he thinks it a distinguishing feature of historical explanation that it be expressed in vague terms. But although historical explanations would, on this ground, be marked off from all

[1] 'Criteria of Explanation in History', *Journal of Philosophy*, 1952, p. 60.
[2] Op. cit., p. 63.

scientific ones as 'non-technical', the same criterion would, of course, admit as specifically historical *all* the explanations given in daily life which are also framed in ordinary language.

Professor Popper, although also approaching the question within the framework of covering law theory, offers a different and more direct answer to it. As we saw in Chapter I, one of the implications which Popper draws from the model as he states it is the necessity of distinguishing between the 'historical' and the 'pure generalizing' sciences. The latter do not explain particular facts. To do this is the task of the historical sciences; and they perform that task by assuming or taking for granted the laws which, ideally, these other sciences discover. According to Popper, "*all* causal explanation of a singular event can be said to be historical in so far as the 'cause' is described by singular initial conditions".[1] It is historical, presumably, because it explains a particular fact—a bit of history—by applying to it a known law. Popper does not, at any rate in the sources indicated, say precisely what such specifically historical explanation is to be contrasted with. But the contrast he has in mind appears to be with explanations achieved by *discovering* rather than assuming the law which governs the facts investigated. There is thus, for him, a pragmatic difference—a difference in the *direction of inquiry*—between historical and non-historical explanation.

Popper's criterion has the merit of distinguishing between historical and non-historical explanation *within* the class marked off by Gardiner as non-technical. Yet his criterion, like Gardiner's, is too broad; for it cuts across the class of technical (i.e. scientific) explanations as well. It would, for instance, classify as historical the explanations given by a chemistry demonstrator of the changed colour of a piece of litmus paper after being dipped in an acid solution. The statement, 'It was dipped in that acid solution', sets out a 'singular initial condition', but it would hardly be regarded as giving anything which we should normally call an historical

[1] 'The Poverty of Historicism', *Economica*, 1945, p. 83. See also *The Open Society*, vol. ii, p. 262.

explanation. For the real work of the explanation is done by a chemical theory which the demonstrator knows how to apply to the case. And although White's analysis was in other ways unsatisfactory, he was surely right to insist that no criterion which allowed an overlap of, say, 'historical' and 'chemical' explanations could be acceptable.

Indeed, as the discussion of the present chapter has suggested, it would be very natural to draw a sharp contrast between historical explanations and *all* theoretical ones. This becomes more obvious if we rephrase the question, 'What is it to give an historical explanation?', as 'What is it to explain something historically?' A theory of the subject matter, as we have seen, may *excuse* an investigator from explaining a thing historically; a specifically historical explanation is given where what is to be explained cannot be understood merely by referring to such systematic general knowledge. We give theoretical explanations where our knowledge of the subject matter allows explanatory interpolation; we give historical ones where no such interpolation is licensed—where we have to refer to the peculiar history of what is to be explained. On this view, it might be noticed, a historical explanation would be distinguished from an applied sociological one—as on Popper's it would not.

In *The Nature of Historical Explanation* Gardiner warns us against thinking that "provided a careful search is conducted, a 'clear and distinct idea' of what historical explanation *is* will somewhere be found".[1] If by this he means that the term 'historical explanation' has no single 'correct' use, I should not want to disagree. I should not want to claim any more for the sense sketched above than that it is close to what we should probably mean if we called one explanation 'historical' by contrast with another, and that the contrast is different in kind from the one sought by White in terms of covering law theory. That there are other uses of the term 'historical explanation', both broader and narrower than this one, I do not doubt.

[1] Op. cit., p. xi.

A common narrower use would require that the explanatory story itself include reference to facts temporally remote from what is explained—a use suggested by Butterfield's observation that the Whig historians "found a historical explanation for the conduct of the Whigs".[1] And a broader one is employed by Gardiner throughout his book, since he generally takes 'historical explanation' to be equivalent to 'explanation found in history books'. Gardiner's broad use may appear to have the advantage of making it possible to say that historians, when they offer explanations, always offer historical explanations; for we could not say this on the narrower interpretations distinguished above. But, as the chapters to follow will help to make clear, if we adopt the broad use of the term, it is unlikely that we shall find any *logical* features according to which all historical explanations can be grouped together as historical. For the explanations found in history books are a logically miscellaneous lot.

[1] *History and Human Relations*, p. 121.

IV

CAUSAL LAWS AND CAUSAL ANALYSIS

1. *The Causal Version of the Model*

So far I have said very little about specifically *causal* explanation. In Chapter II, although causal language was not avoided altogether, our concern was chiefly to test the covering law claims with respect to explanations which were complete in a special sense, and which would not necessarily, or even naturally, be formulated in causal terms. In Chapter III, too, no attempt was made to contrast explanations given by making reference to causal laws with explanations of other kinds. But some defenders of the model have stated their claims explicitly in terms of covering *causal* laws, as if subsumption under these constituted a special case. It may therefore be worth our while, even at the risk of some repetition of points made in a different context of discussion, to ask whether there are any peculiarities about specifically causal explanations which might, or might appear to, count either for or against the argument which has been developed so far.

The causal version of the model, like the broader theory, may be regarded as formulating both a necessary and a sufficient condition of giving an explanation. A. J. Ayer puts the necessary condition claim without qualification when he declares: "every assertion of a particular causal connection involves the assertion of a causal law";[1] and Gardiner, in discussing the stock Humian billiard-ball example, observes: "the force of the word 'because' derives from the fact that a particular case has been seen to satisfy the requirements of a causal law . . . ."[2] Straightforward statements of the sufficient condition claim are less commonly found. But it is not at all

---

[1] *Language, Truth and Logic* (2nd ed.), London, 1948, p. 55.
[2] Op. cit., p. 2; see also p. 114. For other examples, see quotations from Professors Kaufmann and Braithwaite, Chap. I, section 2.

uncommon for philosophers to represent causal laws as having
special explanatory force. Thus C. J. Ducasse, after defining
explanation in terms of subsumption under a 'law of connection', and having added that a mere 'law of correlation' will
not do, goes on to say that laws of the former sort are either
causal or logical.[1] And many contemporary philosophers of
science, with quantum physics in mind, would agree with
Mr. A. P. Ushenko that causal laws alone have "explanatory
virtue".[2]

No doubt many of those who have phrased the covering law
claim in terms of specifically causal laws have used the term
'causal' carelessly. Some have meant no more than 'empirical
laws', by contrast with, say, general principles of logic. Others
have probably had in mind a distinction within the class
of empirical laws, between mere 'probability hypotheses' or
statistical generalizations and genuinely universal laws—for
causal laws are often held to set forth invariable connexions.
But the notion of a causal law is often taken in a more obvious
sense as simply a law expressible in causal language—a law
which would naturally assume the form 'X causes y'. In
assessing the causal version of the covering law model, it is
this latter interpretation which I propose to adopt.

To say that one sort of thing *causes* another to happen is
usually held to mean something more than that phenomena of
the first type are always followed by phenomena of the second.
As M. R. Cohen puts it, in the course of warning social
scientists against philosophers who regard causality as nothing
but repeated succession: "A causal relation asserts more than
mere past coincidence. It affirms that there is some reason
or ground why, whenever the antecedent event occurs, the
consequent must follow."[3]

What sort of 'reason' or 'ground' is envisaged here? Why
are specifically causal connexions especially tight and intelligible? According to one currently popular view, a law of

[1] 'Explanation, Mechanism and Teleology', Feigl and Sellars, *Readings in Philosophical Analysis*, p. 540.
[2] 'The Principles of Causality', *The Journal of Philosophy*, 1953, pp. 85–86.
[3] *The Meaning of Human History*, p. 102.

causal connexion, by contrast with a mere law of observed correlation, derives its necessity from a *logical* connexion between cause and effect, in the light of some accepted general theory of the subject matter. Thus Ryle holds that causal statements are themselves covertly theoretical. Causes, he says, are designated by words which are more heavily 'theory-loaded' than the words which designate their effects; they have as part of their *meaning* an essential theoretical reference.[1] The reason why 'wound', for instance, is the right kind of word to use in indicating the cause of a scar, while 'pain', although also designating an antecedent condition, is not, lies in the fact that it carries the right kind of theoretical load to explain scars—i.e. a medical or physiological one. Similarly, although a red sky is quite incapable of *causing* a fall of rain, a cold front may be said to do so because of the meteorological load of the term concerned.

Such an account of the explanatory force of specifically causal laws has the merit of going beyond a mere statement that causal connexions must be more than instances of uniformly observed sequences. Ryle says both what the 'more' is—a theory—and why it is not always obvious to those who recognize the connexion; and if his analysis held good in all, or even the vast majority of cases, the problem of elucidating the explanatory role of causal laws could simply be referred back to my discussion in the previous chapter of the way theories provide explanations. But it is important for our understanding of causal explanation in history to recognize that Ryle's analysis does not hold good generally. In the discussion to follow, I shall deny that the causal explanations which historians commonly give can be said to require or presuppose corresponding causal laws—for reasons arising out of the peculiarities of causal analysis as well as for reasons of the kind already advanced in non-causal cases. But I shall argue, too, that causes seldom explain their effects by virtue

---

[1] In lectures delivered at Oxford University during Trinity Term, 1952. Ryle's theory has been developed farther by N. R. Hanson in 'Causal Chains', *Mind*, 1955, pp. 289–311.

of some implicit theory—indeed, that they need not explain their effects at all.

It is worth noticing, in this connexion, that the providing of causal explanations has not always been regarded as part of the historian's proper task. Indeed, serious misgivings have often been expressed by philosophers and methodologists of history as to whether the word 'cause' ought to appear in historical writing at all. What is, on the face of it, more curious still, such doubts have been expressed not only by opponents of the covering law model like Oakeshott and Collingwood, but by many of its convinced supporters as well.

Thus, in the bulletin of the American Social Science Research Council already referred to, can be found a warning from Professor Hook to the effect that 'cause' is "an ambiguous and difficult term of varied and complex meaning", which should be used by historians "with circumspection".[1] The warning so impressed his historical colleagues that they concluded that the term 'cause' as used by historians "must be regarded as a convenient figure of speech, describing motives, influences, forces and other antecedent interrelations not fully understood".[2] And two historians, Professors C. A. Beard and A. Vagts, in a minority report, went on to declare that the term "should never be used in written history", being suitable only for "conversations" and "small practical affairs". In his methodological primer for historians, Gottschalk comments caustically: "this is a roundabout admission that the authors of this proposition are somewhat baffled by the problem of causation."[3] Yet he too feels obliged in the end to admit that "the problem of historical causation is still essentially unsolved".

The objection of the idealists is not so much that 'cause' is too loose and slippery a word for 'scientific' history, as that it is, when understood, found to be an irrelevant or inappropriate category. According to Oakeshott, its use betrays an

---

[1] *Bulletin No. 54*, p. 110.   [2] Op. cit., p. 137.
[3] *Understanding History*, Chicago, 1951, p. 223.

anti-historical way of thinking about the subject-matter—an attempt to convert history into a kind of science.[1] For Oakeshott, causal analysis is *too* scientific rather than not scientific enough. The view of Collingwood is similar, although more complicated. Collingwood analyses the concept of causation into three related notions, only one of which is a proper historical category, the others being legitimate and illegitimate extensions of the concept for scientific purposes. According to Collingwood, in so far as we mean anything more by a cause than 'affording someone a motive for doing something' (he calls this 'Sense I'), the notion has no place in historical studies.[2]

Now it is perfectly clear that, no matter what these theorists say, historians do commonly *attempt* to provide causal explanations of what they study. This is a fact which can be verified by the most cursory glance at one or two standard history textbooks. As Mandelbaum has observed: "This acceptance in practice of what is disdained in theory constitutes a paradox worth investigating."[3] In examining the causal version of the model in this chapter I shall, to some extent, be investigating it. For it will be my thesis that once the difference between offering a causal analysis of, and applying causal laws to, a particular happening is appreciated, many of the difficulties which the philosophers in question have seemed to find in the use of the causal concept in history will be seen to disappear.

2. *The Discovery of Causal Laws*

Let us begin by investigating the notion that a causal law is a law of an especially tight and, at the same time, explanatory sort. What should be said in this connexion about a common-sense causal assertion like: 'Dirt causes disease'? It does, indeed, appear that the truth of such a 'law' depends on more than just the observation of a correlation between dirt and disease—at any rate, it *asserts* more than that dirt is always

---

[1] See section 5 below.   [2] *An Essay on Metaphysics*, pp. 285–6.
[3] 'Causal Analysis in History', *Journal of the History of Ideas*, 1942, p. 30.

accompanied by disease. But what exactly are we to say about this 'more'? On the face of it, at any rate, such an example would seem to raise difficulties for Ryle's account of the theoretical background to causal statements. For, if anything, it appears to be the effect word which, in this case, carries the heavier theoretical load. The word 'dirt' is not in any obvious way 'theory-loaded', yet the meaning of the causal statement is clear enough, and it would probably be regarded as true by many people.

It might, I suppose, be argued that the notion of a 'theoretical load' must be taken more subtly than this. For what a word is intended to convey—especially a 'loaded' one—may be dependent in an important way upon its context of utterance. Thus, in the motor-car example of the previous chapter, the term 'oil reservoir' had a very different significance for the assistant mechanic, who understood the lubricating system, and for me, who thought of it only as a receptacle into which oil was put. We might say that there is a contextual dimension to theory-loading, so that a word which ordinarily lacked a theoretical reference might acquire one in the right context. 'Dirt' might be a case in point. The circumstances in which one might say 'Dirt causes disease'—e.g. in a class of probationer nurses, not yet sufficiently proficient in sterile techniques—might be such that the word means more than, say, 'dust'. It might mean something more like 'substance laden with bacteria'.

That an ordinary word like 'dirt' might fluctuate a good deal in its implicit theoretical reference from one context to another is no doubt true, and it is therefore necessary to restate Ryle's theory in such a way that this can be taken into account. Yet I should still want to question the claim that a causal statement like 'Dirt causes disease' could only be said meaningfully, or justifiably, in contexts where one could reasonably claim that a theoretical reference was understood.

A defender of the Rylian account might be willing to go one step farther in the attempt to accommodate examples like the one we are considering. It might be allowed that one could meaningfully say 'Dirt causes disease' without any of the relevant theoretical knowledge (call it 'the germ theory of disease') as long as one did not deny that there must *be* some such connexion between them. Thus the ward helper might learn the same lesson as the student nurses, without learning the medical significance of 'dirt'. For him it is enough to be able to identify dirt in order to get rid of it. The justification for his saying 'Dirt causes disease' is then indirect; it is a matter of a very proper faith in authority. The kernel of Ryle's account would survive, however, in that for *someone* 'dirt' must carry a theoretical load.

Such a defence re-emphasizes the consideration which led to Ryle's analysis: the fact that, even where a person does not know what the 'connexion' between cause and effect is, he at any rate assumes that there is one to be discovered. Any alternative account to the view that the connexion in question is theoretical must elucidate its nature in some other way; it must do more than just return to the simple, Humian 'regularity' analysis which Ryle's notion of a 'theoretical load' supplements to advantage in so many cases. Let me therefore explain why I do not think that the concessions made can render Ryle's account universally applicable, and in what alternative way the notion of 'a connexion' may have to be interpreted.

Let us consider the statement, 'Dirt causes disease', said not by the supervisor of a modern hospital, but by, for example, Florence Nightingale to some of her early helpers. I shall assume that none of them knew the germ theory of disease. Even if this was not true of them, it probably was true of some of their predecessors. Is there no way in which they (or such predecessors) could have arrived at the truth of the causal statement?

It seems to me that Florence Nightingale could have discovered that dirty hospitals caused disease among her patients without necessarily knowing why this was so—at any rate, without knowing the theoretical connexion between the two. Nor does the possibility that she might merely have got this on authority arise. The discovery could have been (and probably was originally in fact) made by observing correlations between dirt and disease in hospitals of the time. It would be noticed that cleaner hospitals had lower, and dirty hospitals had higher, death-rates from disease; and it would be found that when she and her helpers cleaned up a dirty hospital, the disease-rate fell. This is quite sufficient to justify her saying: 'Dirt causes disease.'

Is this to relapse into the position which Ducasse, Cohen, and Ryle all wish (and I think rightly) to avoid: the view that causation is reducible without remainder to correlation; or, to put it in a more precise way, the view that x is the cause of y if whenever x then y? If I had talked only about what Miss Nightingale and her helpers *observed*, there would be some room for such a charge, for, as Ryle has rightly insisted, we cannot discover causes merely by looking—nor, indeed, by *repeated* looking. But there is an additional fact to be taken into account here; for the causal conclusions drawn rested not just on what these women saw, but also on what they found themselves able to *do*. The crucial step in their investigations was the discovery that if they removed the dirt, the disease-rate dropped; if they allowed their sanitary operations to flag, then up it went again. Their quite adequate grounds for concluding that dirt causes disease were that by *manipulating* the dirt-rate, they found themselves able to control the disease-rate.

One important difference between causal candidates which merely satisfy the test of invariable correlation, and those which also meet such a practical test, is this. Having observed that whenever x then y, if I merely know that from an occurrence of x it is safe to predict a y, without knowing the nature of the 'connexion' between them, then I must always be prepared to entertain the hypothesis that *both* x and y are effects of something else. If, for instance, I observe that the birth-rate of white mice in New York is correlated with the divorce-rate of movie stars in California, I must be ready to entertain the hypothesis that both are caused by, say, sun-spot cycles, or the fluctuations of a yet undiscovered element in the atmosphere.[1] This, of course, remains mere hypothesis unless the connexion between them, perhaps in terms of a theory, becomes clear. In some cases, for an initially puzzling correlation of this kind, a satisfactory indirect connexion can eventually be found—as, for instance, between the influx of visitors to seaside resorts and crime waves (both may be caused by 'summer heat'). A direct causal connexion may also sometimes be shown to underly a correlation—as, for instance, in the case of the correlation between the size of rabbit populations and the prevalence of dust storms. In the white mice example we should probably regard it as a waste of time to look for a common cause; we should be content to say that the correlation was just a coincidence. Yet if it were very persistent, it would become less and less satisfactory to say this, and we should feel more and more obliged to look either for a direct or indirect connexion of the kinds mentioned.

Could it be objected that we *do* sometimes say that one phenomenon is the cause of another merely because one is found to be uniformly prior to the other in experience? It seems to me that to say this would generally be regarded (and rightly so) as just the expression of a 'hunch', which required to be confirmed by elucidating the nature of the 'connexion'. It would be more accurate in such cases to say, 'I think x causes y', or 'x probably causes y'. But—and this is the point I wish to emphasize—what we could *not* consistently say is that x does not cause y even though by manipulating x we can control y. If whenever the pest control officer in New York succeeds in reducing the size of the white mice population, the divorce-rate falls in California, then we cannot avoid the conclusion that a change in the birth-rate causes a change in the divorce-rate. And in a particular case, we should have to allow that the cause of the observed change in the divorce-rate was the manipulation of the death-rate—thus applying our knowledge of the causal law.

[1] For a discussion of the problem of distinguishing correlation and causation in the social sciences see M. R. Cohen, op. cit., p. 16.

To deny that agency is, in this way, an *alternative* to theory in validating an alleged causal connexion could only be justified, I think, on the basis of some metaphysical hypothesis of the 'Evil Genius' type. That is, it might be insisted that even if whenever I manipulate x, y alters in the relevant way, this may still be due to some unknown 'third thing', for instance, the synchronizing activities of a Cartesian demon who delights to deceive us—to make us think that we are in control. But such an extravagant hypothesis deserves no place in our analysis. Indeed, metaphysical arguments could just as easily be found for saying that we can never be sure on *any* (e.g. even theoretical) grounds that one thing is the cause of another. The metaphysical objection may seem to derive some force from the possibility that, on some occasion, my attempt to control a certain y by manipulating a certain x may not work. But this is just an aspect of the general corrigibility of empirical statements. I see no reason to doubt that a causal statement of the form 'x causes y', may, in some cases, be confirmed to the point where the possibility that, when someone has produced an x, a y will not follow, is only a logical possibility. For anyone but a metaphysician, i.e. for a scientist, historian, or plain man, it would therefore be unreasonable to take the metaphysical way out.[1]

In *An Essay on Metaphysics* Collingwood points out that, in one of the uses of the term 'cause' (he calls it 'Sense II'), the cause of a thing is the *handle* by means of which we can control it; it is "an event or state of things which it is in our power to produce or prevent, and by producing or preventing which we can produce or prevent that whose cause it is said to be".[2] Thus, to quote some of his examples: "The cause of malaria is the bite of a mosquito; the cause of a boat's sinking is her being overloaded; the cause of books going mouldy is their being in a damp room; the cause of a man's sweating is a dose of aspirin. . . ."[3] Such causes, Collingwood adds,

---

[1] The sentence which originally ended this paragraph has been deleted in response to a criticism of Professor John Passmore

[2] p. 296.   [3] p. 299.

always depend for their operation upon *conditiones sine quibus non*.

There are, however, two ways of interpreting Collingwood's point. On what might be called the 'weak' interpretation, his doctrine of 'the handle' might be regarded as merely calling attention to a practical condition which must be satisfied by any causal candidate. If he is right about it, what falls under the antecedent clause of a law cannoṭ be a cause—and, *a fortiori*, the law cannot be a causal one—unless the condition specified is a manipulable one. This has often been dismissed as a correct, but not very important, observation about our 'ordinary' use of the word 'cause'.

But in the present instance, I am not just saying that manipulability is often one of the criteria to be satisfied before calling something a cause. What I claim is that there are cases where Collingwood's 'handle' *replaces* Ryle's requirement that there be a theoretical connexion between cause and effect: that if a certain condition satisfies the practical test, then that is enough to give it causal status. Let us call this the *strong* interpretation of Collingwood's doctrine of the 'handle'. Even in the strong use, of course, there are still, in theory, *conditiones sine quibus non*; for causal laws only indicate sufficient conditions, *ceteris paribus*, of what falls under their apodoses.[1] But in contexts where we speak with point of the discovery and use of causal laws, the notion of there being additional necessary conditions is swallowed up in the assumption of a normal application situation for the law—the details of which we need not have gone into. They are taken into account by the context of inquiry—e.g. British hospitals in the nineteenth century.

In the light of this account of the way causal laws are often discovered and used, it would be rather odd to regard them as invariably explanatory. For in so far as a causal law—one which we should naturally express in the form 'x causes y'— is arrived at by manipulation, we may expect it to be formulated for just that kind of situation where we should admit that

[1] On the use of '*ceteris paribus*' see Note B, p. 170.

no explanatory connexion between cause and effect is known. As Collingwood himself pointed out, the criterion of 'the handle' (in what I have called the 'strong' use) is appropriate to the practical rather than the theoretical (i.e. explanatory) sciences. Thus, although it is necessary to insist, with Ducasse, Cohen, Ryle, and others, that causation is not reducible to mere correlation—for it is always more than this—it is important to recognize that it may very well be something less than an explanatory connexion between events. It may only be (let us call it) a *practical* connexion; and in such cases, we cannot expect the causal law, when applied to a particular case falling under it, to have much more explanatory force than an ordinary empirical generalization. For we have no 'insight' into the connexion; there is no analysis of the case, no reduction of a gross and opaque connexion to transparent, 'hat-doffing' ones.

3. *The Selection of Causal Conditions*

I have argued that there is nothing about the notion of a 'causal law', in so far as we mean any law which could be expressed in causal language, which would make subsumption under one invariably explanatory. If we turn now to the companion claim that knowledge of a causal law is at any rate a necessary condition of giving a causal explanation, we shall find even less reason for allowing it—especially in history. For in typical historical cases, any causal law extracted from the historian's particular causal explanation will appear just as artificial and just as innocent of independent justification as the non-causal examples discussed in Chapter II. The test for Florence Nightingale's causal assertion was: 'Repeat the cause and the effect should follow.' No such test is relevant to an assertion like 'The cause of Louis XIV's unpopularity was his foreign wars'. For the truth of the historian's assertion does not depend on the particular causal connexion being an instance of a causal routine.

If a particular causal explanation does not represent what happened as an instance of some causal routine, what should be said about its logical structure? On what grounds does an historian represent something as 'the cause' when examining a particular state of affairs? In answering these questions, it is helpful to distinguish between two sorts of tests which would seem to be applicable to any causal candidate. On the one hand, the historian must be able to show that the condition called the cause was really necessary, i.e. that without it what is to be explained would not have happened. He must also be able to show that there is some reason for singling out the condition in question from among the other necessary conditions, which, since what is to be explained did in fact happen, may be presumed to amount to a sufficient set. These might be called the *inductive* and *pragmatic* tests of causal selection. Causes, that is, must be important *to* the inquirer as well as important *for* the effect. Let me try to bring out briefly some of the features of each of these two kinds of importance.

Collingwood's doctrine of 'the handle', in what I have called its 'weak' interpretation, formulates one pragmatic criterion which is often applied. The historian will normally be concerned to indicate as causes those conditions which were humanly important because under human control; and causes will thus often appear in historical writing as what was done by the historical agents who are mentioned in the historian's narrative. It is important to add, of course, that the 'handle' test would apply just as well to cases where we are referred to what was left *un*-done; for historical causes are often non-occurrences, absences, failures to do what could have been done.

In accepting Collingwood's point, there is no need to push it to the paradoxical extreme which he himself allowed—that the cause must always be the sort of thing which would have been a possible handle for the *speaker* (or writer). All we need to say is that a cause is selected in the light of a certain kind of inquiry.[1] This is sufficient explanation of the puzzle which

---

[1] As Gardiner puts it, 'cause' is a function of language level (op. cit., p. 10). My remarks here are only intended to supplement Gardiner's discussion in Part III, section 4.

leads Collingwood to assert his doctrine of 'the relativity of causes': the doctrine that the cause of, say, an explosion, will be different for a chemist, a night-watchman, and an investigator from the City Hall. If a dispute were to develop between these three as to what condition was *really* the cause, it would have to be pointed out to them that it depended partly on what kind of steps they were interested in discovering toward avoiding such disasters in future. If an historian, writing later about the explosion, takes up the point of view of one or other of these kinds of agents—he may, for instance, be writing 'administrative history'—then his selection of the causal condition will be governed accordingly. If he is, on the other hand, writing general history, and is therefore not involved in the hypothetical controversy, he may feel obliged to list more than one cause. But he would find it difficult to ignore the practical criterion for the selection of causes altogether.

Collingwood's analysis of the pragmatic test for causes is not exhaustive, however. For many other practical considerations besides manipulability could be elicited from our ordinary use of causal language. A causal explanation is often, for instance, designed to show what went wrong; it focuses attention not just on what was or could have been done, but on what *should* or *should not* have been done by certain historical agents. Thus, selecting the causal condition sometimes cannot be divorced from assigning blame.[1] The close connexion between the two is recognized by Halévy when, in writing about the fluctuations in the price of wheat in England in 1816–17, he says: "an attempt was made to prove that the Corn Bill was the cause of these wild fluctuations. But to bring forward such a charge was tantamount to maintaining that the Bill was ineffective, and had failed to fulfil its authors' intentions."[2] It is significant, in this connexion, that historians often use expressions like 'was responsible for' when they

[1] The above point may be added to what is said in Chap. V, sections 2 and 5, about the way explanation in the humanities goes beyond anything covering law theorists would accept as 'scientific'.

[2] *A History of the English People in the Nineteenth Century*, 2nd edn. (revised), tr. by E. I. Watkin, London, 1949, vol. ii, p. 61.

want to put into other words conclusions which they would also be prepared to frame in causal language.

Thus, if, with a recent writer on the subject, we were to ask: "Can history really show by its method that Hitler's invasion of Poland was *the* cause of the war?", we should be wise to clarify the question before trying to answer it.[1] Two historians who argue, for instance, whether it was Hitler's invasion of Poland or Chamberlain's pledge to defend it which caused the outbreak of the Second World War are not just arguing about whether these were necessary conditions of what happened. Nor, indeed, is it likely that they are at odds about which of these candidate-causes was a manipulable condition—since, in an inter-subjective sense, both clearly were. They are trying, rather, to settle the question of who was to blame. In such cases, it should be noticed, there is an *essential* connexion between assigning responsibility and attributing causal status. The point is not that we cannot hold an agent responsible for a certain happening unless his action can be said to have caused it. It is rather that, unless we are prepared to hold the agent responsible for what happened, we cannot say that his action *was* the cause. The pragmatic criterion is not just something added to a causal judgement already made on other grounds; for that judgement is itself, in part, the judgement that a certain condition deserves special attention.

There are many other pragmatic reasons for selecting conditions as causal ones. Causes are often, for instance, the initially mysterious or hidden conditions—the ones which still remain to be discovered after we have gained a preliminary knowledge of a situation. Professor MacIver makes a similar, although not identical, point when he says that the causal condition is often a 'precipitant'.[2] It is what has to be added to certain other conditions already present—like the spark which ignites an explosion in a powder factory.

To be a 'precipitant' a condition need not be the last one

---

[1] M. C. Swabey, *The Judgment of History*, New York, 1954, p. 26.
[2] *Social Causation*, Boston, 1952, p. 161.

to come into existence, for it is enough generally that it appear as an intruder—a foreign element—in the situation envisaged. As MacIver puts it: "The crucial events regarded as causes are assigned this role because they are represented as interferences with normal conditions."[1] Thus a storm is the cause of a traffic snarl because it blew trees across the roadway. In the language of the social scientist: "The presumption is that a system is operating in a manner congenial to its self-perpetuation until something intervenes. . . ."[2] In historical contexts, the point would simply be that the causal condition is an unexpected one in that particular context. If the cause is a non-occurrence, this requirement would, of course, be inverted: the causal non-occurrence would be something that was to be expected, but which did not occur. It was not a cause of the Second World War that Hitler failed to be struck by lightning on 31 August 1939.

A large-scale attempt to elicit the pragmatic criteria employed in causal analysis in history would be beyond the scope of the present discussion, although it is a project well worth undertaking for its own sake. I have tried only to indicate the sort of thing which might be expected to emerge from a more thorough study, and to show how this aspect of causal analysis raises special difficulties for any attempt to generalize the historian's causal statement as a law. For even a cursory study of the matter seems to me to show that causal explanation does not just *happen* in a great many cases to fall short of the standard of completeness employed in Chapter II. It shows, rather, that such explanation is *necessarily* incomplete if that standard is accepted; for the very notion of 'discovering the cause' requires the *isolation* of some condition or conditions. The resulting contrast is part of what is demanded by a causal 'Why?'

Covering law theorists who agree that, since historical causes are usually only especially important necessary conditions of their effects, it would be misleading to say that the historian's causal conclusion was warranted by a covering

----

[1] Op. cit., p. 186.   [2] Op. cit., p. 173.

causal law, may nevertheless be tempted to argue that his conclusion requires a law of another kind. For it may be thought that in order to satisfy the second, the *inductive*, test of causal selection, it will be necessary to show that without an event of type *x*—the cause—an event of type *y*—the effect— could not have happened. And this may appear to be equivalent to appealing to a law linking effect to necessary condition: a law which might naturally be expressed in the form, 'Only if *x* then *y*'.[1] Such 'laws of necessary condition' would not, of course, render predictable what is to be explained; and to allow that mere subsumption of *x* and *y* under such a law counts as explanation would represent a considerable departure from the original claims of Popper, Hempel, and Gardiner. Yet it may be felt that in insisting that *some* kind of law is required by the explanation, the most important feature of covering law theory is nevertheless retained.

It is important to recognize how seriously such an analysis would misrepresent what may be presumed to be the historian's meaning if he said that the condition he selects as cause was necessary for the happening he wishes to explain. We must remember, as always, that he is talking about particular happenings in a quite definite historical situation. When he says that *y* would not have happened without *x*, he does not mean that only in situations where there is an *x*-type event can you expect a *y*-type. He means that in that *particular situation*, if everything else remained the same, the *y* which in fact occurred would not have done so; or, at any rate, that it would have been different in important respects. The law, 'Only if *x* then *y*', might therefore be quite false, without the historian's conclusion having to be withdrawn. As we saw in Chapter II, there may, for instance, be a number of things which Louis XIV might have done to make himself unpopular

---

[1] Mr. D. Gasking, for instance, points out to historians that ". . . the simplest kind of general law which might be assumed in an explanation is of one or other of two basic types. They are of the form: Whenever you get *A* you get *B* (*A* is a sufficient condition of *B*), and Whenever you don't get *A* you don't get *B* (*A* is a necessary condition of *B*)." 'The Historian's Craft and Scientific History', *Historical Studies Australia and New Zealand*, 1950, p. 116.

besides pursuing the policies he actually did. But the question whether the effect could have been brought about in other ways is not directly relevant to the historian's judgement that, in the particular situation under examination, the cause was necessary.

It would be an exaggeration, however, to say that this question is entirely irrelevant; for if there was a reasonable chance of y happening anyway, even without x, then it would begin to be questionable to call x the cause of y. If, for instance, z would have been a satisfactory substitute for x, and the situation could be shown to be one in which z was not at all unlikely, then the causal status of x would probably come under review. Thus Collingwood, in denying that the length of Cleopatra's nose can be considered a genuine cause of the Roman Empire's taking the course it subsequently took, castigates what he calls "a bankruptcy of historical method which in despair of genuine explanation acquiesces in the most trivial causes for the vastest effects".[1] But why, exactly, does the nose in question fall short of full causal status? It is not because in any obvious sense it is too small a thing to have caused such a 'vast' effect. A causal condition may, in fact, be as small as you please, as long as it is *crucial*. But to be crucial (a notion which includes the pragmatic criterion), a causal condition must be genuinely necessary in the situation envisaged. And it seems obvious enough that Cleopatra's nose falls short of causal status because the historian's general knowledge of the situation in which the Roman Empire grew is such that he believes that it would have taken much the same course if Cleopatra had never existed.

The point which requires emphasis is that, whether or not the historian concludes that the suggested cause was a necessary condition of what he wishes to explain, his argument for the conclusion he in fact reaches need not raise the question whether the condition in question was a *generally* necessary one for events of the type to be explained; for the historian's explanatory problem is not to represent a particular causal connexion as an instance of a recurring one. He does not ask

[1] *The Idea of History*, pp. 80–81.

himself, 'What causes y's?'; he asks, 'What is the cause of
this y?'—and he asks this about a y in a determinate situation.
The conclusion that x was necessary for the occurrence of y
in that situation will, in fact, usually require an exercise of
judgement similar to the one discussed in Chapter II (although
the question is no longer whether certain conditions formed a
sufficient set). It is true that the historian must be *certain* that
without x, y could not have happened, if he is to say without
qualification that x was the cause of y. But there is no need to
assume that the only way he could arrive at such certainty is
by knowing a law of the 'only if' form. As historical methodologists have often pointed out, what the historian has to do
is 'think away' the suggested cause in order to *judge* what
difference its non-occurrence would have made in the light
of what else he knows about the situation studied. If any
qualifying phrase is to be attached to the historian's conclusion
it would read, not 'other things being equal', but *'the situation
being what it was'*—indicating that other mentioned and un-
mentioned features of the particular situation have been taken
into account in arriving at the causal conclusion.

If the causal explanation were seriously challenged on its
inductive side, it might indeed become necessary to bring in,
bit by bit, all the data which in Chapter II were represented
as constituting a complete explanation rather than a causal
one. This is not to say that, after all, we must enlarge our
conception of a cause to that of a sufficient condition rather
than a merely necessary one. It is rather that, if pressed to
show conclusively that x *was* necessary, the historian might
have to specify what, in fact, the other conditions were—i.e.
to rebut the suggestion that even without x they constituted
a sufficient set.

4. *Causal Laws as Generalizations*

In the preceding sections I have called attention to important features of two quite different kinds of causal inquiries:
those in which the investigator seeks to establish general
causal connexions—causal laws—and those in which he seeks

to discover the cause of a particular happening in a determinate, concrete historical situation. And I have denied that the second sort of inquiry need be related to the first in the sense that it applies what the first sort of inquiry discovers.

It may perhaps be felt that although it is true that historians seldom have to deal with instances of causal routines, and that the causal version of the model on its necessary condition side is therefore misleading, my account of the discovery of causal laws does less than justice to the sufficient condition claim. And I must indeed admit that the reasons for doubting the explanatory force of causal laws set out in section 2 need not always hold. A statement of what was at first merely an observed correlation, for instance, could be raised to the status of a causal law by bringing in sufficient theoretical considerations to establish the connexion between cause and effect. The mere *observation*, 'Whenever we find dirt we find disease', although not a causal law, might attain causal force by the discovery of the germ theory of disease. Causal laws may also in some cases be *directly* derivable from theoretical knowledge, without any empirical observation of 'cases'—the 'laws' then showing their origin by being more naturally expressed in the subjunctive mood. An example of such a law might be: 'Sustained nuclear radiation *would cause* genetic deterioration of living beings.' But the fact that a causal law *can* be theory-backed does not reinstate the sufficient condition claim. It does not ensure that if a specifically causal law is 'applied', it must provide an explanation of what falls under it. And it was the purpose of my discussion of the special, experimental case to show that this *general* claim of covering law theory in its causal version cannot be sustained.

Our investigation has, in fact, shown that there are *three* quite different cases to be distinguished when we ask about the nature of 'causal connexion'—or, at any rate, there are three different ways an alleged causal connexion might have to be argued for. For the connexion could be established by reference to manipulative experience, by reference to a logical connexion in terms of some general theory, or by reference to other conditions in a determinate situation which allow the judgement that a certain condition was crucial (both necessary and important).[1] The third way, which requires neither prior experimental nor theoretical knowledge of such connexions, is the standard historical case. Such dicta as F. S. C. Northrop's that "causal necessity or determinism in history is only possible in a deductively formulated social science which has a theoretical dynamics" must be regarded as the recommendation of a reformer rather than an account of the way causal inquiry in history actually goes.[2]

It may be worth pointing out in this connexion that causal *laws*, as well as particular, historical causal connexions, may sometimes be established without either experimental or theoretical justification. Indeed, the relation of 'support' between laws and the particular connexions falling under them, is at times precisely the *opposite* of the one envisaged by covering law theory; for in many cases discovery of individual causal connexions *precedes* the formulation of causal laws, the laws—shocking though it may be to say it—requiring prior knowledge of the particular cases, rather than the cases requiring support of the covering causal law.

How, for instance, might we in practice arrive at a causal conclusion like 'Speed causes road accidents'? Would it not be *by generalization from a number of particular causal diagnoses* of the form: 'The cause of this accident was excessive speed'? The general causal statement is just the sort of thing that a public safety officer might use as a warning, and it could not properly be said unless he could point to a number of cases on record, each standing on its own logical feet—i.e. to individual causal connexions independently validated. Perhaps the same law could have been reached experimentally (which, in this case would be a rather cruel business), or even derived from theoretical knowledge (which is, in this case, unlikely). But in at any rate a great number of contexts where we should be

---

[1] As the discussion of section 6 will show, this threefold distinction does not coincide with Collingwood's division of 'cause' into three 'senses'.

[2] *The Logic of the Sciences and the Humanities*, London, 1947, p. 260.

likely to *use* such causal laws, the laws not only *could*, but *would*, be generalizations from knowledge of particular causal connexions arrived at by an exercise of judgement. We should only advance to asserting the law in addition to the individual diagnoses if the same cause turned up repeatedly in the kind of investigation concerned.

In *The Problem of Historical Knowledge* Mandelbaum asserts that "the formulation of scientific laws depends upon causal analysis" rather than causal analysis upon laws[1]—a claim which both Hempel and Gardiner have attacked as a naïve attempt to ignore what Hume proved about causation.[2] It should be clear that my own claim here is quite different from this. It is limited to the kind of causal laws exemplified above; and such laws would scarcely find a place in a list of the discoveries of, say, chemists and physicists. They might, however, appear among the findings of the *social* sciences; and it would not be very surprising to come upon an article in a medical journal assembling evidence by way of cases, independently judged, in support of an assertion like 'Injections cause tumours' (for in spite of the bad jokes commonly made at its expense, medicine is not *just* a practical science). An exactly parallel case in history would be a law like 'Tyranny causes revolution'. Such a 'law' would almost certainly be a causal *generalization*.

The suggestion of generalization from cases independently discovered comes out even more strongly when we consider laws of the form: 'The cause of y is x' (where these symbols stand for types, not particulars). For it is difficult to see how this stronger form of causal law could be established experimentally; and in most cases, theoretical support would not be available to show that the effect cannot happen without the indicated cause. One of Collingwood's examples, 'The cause of malaria is the bite of a mosquito', shows how such theoretical support may sometimes function, for it is, in this case, our general knowledge of the nature of the disease, and the way

---

[1] pp. 236–8.
[2] Gardiner, op. cit., p. 84; Hempel, op. cit., p. 461; Crawford, op. cit., p. 164.

the virus must reach the blood-stream, that allows us to regard the bite as a *generally* necessary condition. But what about 'The cause of road accidents is speed', or 'The cause of war is greed'?

It seems to me that where no theoretical backing is available for them, such 'laws' can only be interpreted as generalizations, and perhaps not even as universal in intention. They merely summarize a trend, observed in the particular cases, toward the isolation of one sort of condition as especially noteworthy. The law, 'The cause of malaria is the bite of a mosquito', tells us there is only one way to get malaria. But the 'law', 'The cause of road accidents is speed', cannot plausibly be interpreted in this way; it tells us only that speed is a particularly common or important condition of such accidents. If this is so, however, the explanatory force of the law is obviously nil when we come to investigate a particular accident, for we have to discover independently whether in that particular case the usual cause was operative or not. Such a law can be no more than suggestive in the search for the actual cause; it merely reminds the historian that (e.g.) on many occasions the cause of war has been found to be greed, so that it is worth his while to be on the lookout for this factor as a possible cause.

It is worth noticing that if laws of the form 'the cause of y is x', strictly interpreted, *were* used by historians in giving their explanations, we should have to say that the historian would know the explanation of what he studied without bothering to find out by historical research what the antecedent conditions actually were. For the existence of the causal condition could simply be retrodicted by means of the law— as we should have no hesitation in doing, for instance, in the malaria case. In the historical example discussed above, the most that would be left for the historian's investigation of the particular case would be the detailed description of the greed which caused this particular war. But this of course bears no resemblance to the problem which has to be solved in typical historical cases. For even if the historian should *find* greed among the antecedents of a particular war, he would *still* not know the explanation of the war in question; he would *still* have to ask whether greed was in this case the cause.

Laws of the form, 'The cause of *y* is *x*', are in fact seldom likely to be available to the historian; they are certainly less likely to be known than laws of the form, '*X* causes *y*'. Since even where they were available, they would have a very dubious explanatory force, this need not be thought to create any difficulty for the giving of causal explanations in history— a fact sometimes lost sight of in discussions of the special problems of causal inquiry in history. M. R. Cohen, for instance, points out that just as we cannot ask for *the* cause of disease, so we cannot ask for *the* cause of historical phenomena like trade disturbances; for the class of things in question, he says, is too heterogeneous for us to expect to find a common cause.[1] In the light of what has just been said, however, it will be seen that this, although it may be true, is no problem whatever for an historian who wishes to explain a particular trade disturbance.

Nor would the explanatory force of laws of the kind discussed be increased by framing them in terms of a plurality of causes. Perhaps an historian would not regard it as part of his proper task to give an answer to a question like 'What are the causes of war?' Yet it might very well be regarded as belonging to the sphere of the generalizing social sciences. Such a case, however, would illustrate very badly the general positivist thesis regarding the proper relationship between historian and sociologist: that the historian digs up facts, passes them to the social scientist so that he can make laws out of them, and return them for application by the historian in particular explanations. For in the case envisaged, the 'facts' which the historian would deliver for the purpose of generalization would already be explained: they would consist of particular explanations of particular wars. What the generalization would add to the historian's diagnoses is merely to elicit any general trend there may be toward the selection of certain

---

[1] 'Causation and its Application to History', *Journal of the History of Ideas*, 1942, p. 17, n. 2.

conditions as causes. It is not to depreciate the usefulness of such generalizations to point out that the resulting law can scarcely provide the justification for the individual explanations upon which it rests.

5. *Misgivings about Causal Language in History*

In the light of the foregoing discussion, what can be said to ease the misgivings of those who question the propriety of causal terminology in historical writing? It seems to me that the objections of both the opponents and the supporters of the covering law model owe a great deal of their plausibility to their failure to take into account some of the features of causal inquiries which have just been examined.

Is 'cause' a loose or vague term? Those who, like Beard and Vagts, have urged its abandonment have generally rested their case on the fact that singular causal statements made by historians commonly come to grief when they are generalized as causal laws. They see that from most of the conditions which historians designate as causes, the effect could not safely have been predicted. But why should they have expected otherwise? It can surely only be because the illicit assumption is made that a cause, when fully stated, must always be a sufficient condition of its effect. This assumption has been reinforced from time to time by what philosophers have had to say. Thus Mandelbaum, in a careful, formal statement, defines the cause of an event as "the complete set of those events without which the event would not have occurred, or whose non-existence or non-occurrence would have made some difference to it".[1] But this, as we have seen, is far from being the usual sense of the term in history. Indeed, even in contexts where causal laws are formulated, the notion is not screwed up as tightly as this, since the causes in question are only sufficient conditions, *ceteris paribus*.

There are two ways in which reformers might hope to deal with the supposed 'looseness' of causal language in history. It has been proposed by O. Neurath, for instance, that his-

---

[1] 'Causal Analysis in History', *Journal of the History of Ideas*, 1942, p. 39.

torians should abandon the claim that they discover causes; they should say only that certain events and conditions 'arise out of' other events and conditions.[1] A quite different suggestion may be gleaned from the view of those who, like M. R. Cohen, regard a 'tight' sense of the word 'cause' as strictly correct, but who go on to allow that there is a looser sense which is appropriate in "popular discourse".[2] The suggestion would seem to be that the more carefully, i.e. 'scientifically', history is written, the more likely it is that we shall find 'cause' used to designate a set of sufficient conditions.

Should a 'tight' sense of the word be adopted in order to improve the precision of historical writing? There are right and wrong reasons for resisting such a programme. One of the wrong ones was given by Collingwood when he attacked the tight sense as self-contradictory (he called it 'Sense III', and claimed to find it in the literature of the theoretical sciences of nature). Collingwood's argument is a development of Russell's complaint that in order to be strictly sufficient for predicting the effect, cause and effect must be *coincident* in space and time—so that the cause becomes identical with the effect, and hence no cause at all.[3] But the tight sense defined by Mandelbaum and Cohen would be subject to Collingwood's and Russell's strictures only if 'sufficient' were defined in a metaphysically absolute way inappropriate to a 'scientific' use. All we need mean by the set of sufficient conditions (as I suggested in Chapter II), is those from which, on the criteria we ordinarily accept as appropriate in the subject-matter concerned, the event could justifiably have been predicted.

The right reason for rejecting the suggestion is pragmatic;

---

[1] 'Foundations of the Social Sciences', *International Encyclopedia of the Unified Sciences*, Chicago, 1944, vol. 2, No. 1, pp. 20–21. Gardiner mentions this, op. cit., p. 9.

It is interesting to note that in a second bulletin of the Social Science Research Council on theory of history, historians are reported to be "in general agreed that it would be extremely difficult to devise workable substitutes for such terms as 'cause' and 'causality' " (*The Social Sciences in Historical Study*, New York, 1954, p. 12).

[2] 'Causation and its Application to History', *Journal of the History of Ideas*, 1942, p. 19.

[3] Russell, *Mysticism and Logic*, p. 187; Collingwood, *Essay on Metaphysics*, pp. 314–15. Gardiner notes this argument, op. cit., p. 8.

for the so-called 'loose' sense of 'cause' already has a useful employment in history. Historians use the notion to draw attention to some necessary condition which, for one reason or another, is considered important in the context of writing. To say that the word is ordinarily used 'vaguely' or 'loosely' is thus misleading. We should say rather that the term has its own peculiar logic, which happens to be different from that invented for it by some philosophers. It cannot be tightened up in either the metaphysical or scientific ways without changing its function; and the reformed notion could not, in any case, be employed without bringing historical narrative to a halt. Nor need we be tempted by Neurath's curious linguistic recommendation; for this loses its point if we recognize the fact that there is nothing *wrong* with calling anything less than a set of sufficient conditions a 'cause'.

The objection that causal analysis in history is not scientific enough thus arises, at least in part, out of a failure to appreciate the point of causal language. What about the counter-objection that explanation in terms of causes is *too* scientific? According to Oakeshott, the search for causes is anti-historical in conception; it belongs to the practical (for him 'scientific') problem of prediction and control. To pick out causes is somehow to falsify the concrete nature of the historian's subject-matter; to divert attention from the actual course of events which it is the historian's business to reconstruct from the evidence. In taking such a view, Oakeshott has the qualified support of some members of the historical profession. Professor Renier, for instance, believes that "the normal interpretation of causation contains dangerous elements which threaten the basic quality of the historical narrative".[1] And Teggart, too, regards historical narration and the search for causes as incompatible tasks—although, being a campaigner for 'scientific' history, this leads him to take a jaundiced view of narrative rather than of causal analysis.[2]

What really bothers Oakeshott comes out more clearly if we

---

[1] *History, Its Purpose and Method*, London, 1950, p. 181.
[2] 'Causation in Historical Events', *Journal of the History of Ideas*, 1942, p. 6.

ask what he regards as the proper historical alternative to causal explanation. As we noted in Chapter III, he does not deny that the historian explains at all. It is rather that "history accounts *for* change by means of a full account *of* change. The relation *between* events", he says, "is always other events, and it is established in history by a full relation *of* the events." According to Oakeshott, "The conception of cause is thus replaced by the exhibition of a world of events intrinsically related to one another in which no *lacuna* is tolerated".[1]

That something correct and important is here being said I should not want to question. But, in the light of my discussion in the present chapter, the sharp contrast which Oakeshott draws between causal explanation and discovering the actual course of events is surely misconceived. Oakeshott assumes that to assign a cause to an event is to bring that event under a law. True, he does not explicitly say this, but he does define 'cause' for scientific purposes as "the minimum antecedent circumstances sufficient to account for an *example* of a *generalized* result".[2] And by contrast with the inapplicability of the causal category to history, he says that it is "possible in science only because the world of scientific experience is a world, not of events but of instances".[3] He concludes: "the strict conception of cause breaks down as the explanatory principle in historical experience, because it contradicts the postulated character of the historical past. . . ."[4]

It is the relegation of the discovery of causes to the world of 'instances' which reveals the source of the difficulty. For if all causal inquiry was like that experimentation which yields knowledge of causal laws—general causal relationships—Oakeshott's criticism would have some force. But, as I have shown, to give and defend a causal explanation in history is scarcely ever to bring what is explained under a law, and almost always involves a descriptive account, a narrative, of the actual course of events, in order to justify the judgement

---

[1] Op. cit., p. 143.　　　　　　　[2] Op. cit., p. 211. My italics.
[3] Op. cit., p. 127. Gardiner notes the objection briefly, op. cit., p. 30.
[4] Op. cit., p. 133.

that the condition indicated was indeed the cause. Finding the
cause of an historical event is thus no *substitute* for knowing
exactly what happened—which Oakeshott rightly regards as
an essential mark of historical inquiry. Indeed, it involves a
judgement which depends on knowing just that.

It is true that in the explanatory statement which arises out
of this detailed knowledge, one or a few conditions are picked
out as 'the cause'. But this does not amount to opening a
'*lacuna*'; nor does it confer upon the causal condition any
mysterious ontological priority.[1] It merely satisfies certain
pragmatic criteria of importance which are superimposed upon,
but do not replace, the inductive requirement that the causal
condition be a necessary one. If Oakeshott were to object
further (as I think he would) that to select any conditions at all
as of more importance than the rest is to allow an intrusion of
the practical into an 'historical world' where such considerations do not belong, I can only resist his *a priori* conception
of what the historian should be trying to do when he explains
a thing—i.e. write history from no point of view whatever.[2]
He is doubtless right to insist that *all* the conditions of an
historical event are necessary, and that the making of distinctions on grounds of importance must not be allowed to obscure
this truth.[3] But that necessary conditions are all necessary is,
after all, no more than a (perhaps useful) tautology.

A misunderstanding of the difference between causal laws
and causal analysis seems to me also to lie behind Collingwood's restriction of the *sense* of 'cause' which is properly
employed in history. Like Oakeshott, Collingwood believes
that in using the notion there is a danger that the historian
may be tempted to slide away from the proper historical task
into something like scientific interests. But this will only
happen, he contends, if the historian uses the word in the

---

[1] Renier deplores the "feeling that a cause occupies a position superior in
reality to its effect" (op. cit., pp. 181 and 183–4).

[2] I offer further reasons for denying that the historian's approach is divorced
from a 'practical' one in Chap. V, section 4.

[3] ". . . every historical event is necessary, and it is impossible to distinguish
between the importance of necessities" (op. cit., p. 129).

wrong sense. For according to Collingwood, there are three senses of 'cause', and the only proper use of the word in history is in Sense I: the sense in which one person can cause another to act in a certain way by providing him with a motive for acting so.[1] Sense II he defines as "an event or state of things by producing or preventing which we can produce or prevent that whose cause it is said to be". Sense III he defines thus:

> . . . that which is 'caused' is an event or state of things, and its 'cause' is another event or state of things standing to it in a one-one relation of causal priority: i.e. a relation of such a kind that (a) if the cause happens or exists the effect must also happen or exist, even if no further conditions are fulfilled, (b) the effect cannot happen or exist unless the cause happens or exists, (c) in some sense which remains to be defined, the cause is prior to the effect. . . .[2]

These three senses Collingwood regards as related by historical derivation from each other. Sense II is derived from Sense I by extending the notion of an effect from the actions of human beings to the behaviour of anything whatever. Sense III is derived from Sense II by tightening the connexion between cause and effect to one of logical necessity, and making the relation between cause and effect one-one.

Collingwood represents Sense II as the one appropriate for the practical sciences of nature; it is the sense employed in the discovery of causal laws by experimentation (as discussed in section 2 above). To say that the historian never uses the notion of 'cause' in this sense is, perhaps, a pardonable exaggeration; for, as I have argued, it is true that his explanations are scarcely ever the applications of causal laws. Yet, as I pointed out earlier, there is a weak as well as a strong interpretation which might be placed upon Collingwood's criterion of the 'handle', and in the weak interpretation this criterion is very often applied by the historian in selecting one from a number of necessary conditions as important. Collingwood's

---

[1] This sense is further discussed in Chap. V, section 7. I do not here question Collingwood's speaking of 'senses' of the word 'cause', although it seems to me preferable to speak of ways of establishing a causal connexion.

[2] *An Essay on Metaphysics*, p. 285–6.

Sense II is therefore open to further analysis. In so far as he means a cause which is sufficient, *ceteris paribus*, then this sense is an uncommon, uncharacteristic one in historical studies. But if he simply means a cause selected because it is a manipulable necessary condition in a determinate situation, then it is in quite common use. Let us call the latter, historical sense, Sense II*a*.

Like Oakeshott, Collingwood is suspicious of any attempt to represent the historian as applying knowledge of general causal connexions in historical cases. It is part of his argument against the historical propriety of Sense II that in this sense "every causal proposition is a general proposition", whereas in Sense I every one is individual.[1] In Sense II, he concludes, "it would be nonsense to inquire after the cause of any individual thing as such". While I see no reason to agree with the latter conclusion, I think it is true, at any rate, that in Sense II*a*, a causal proposition need not assert a causal connexion which can be generalized.

Collingwood's Sense III is a very queer fish. As I have already remarked, it involves a sense of 'sufficient condition' which is tightened up in a metaphysical way. It also, as stated, makes the cause retrodictable from the effect. At the same time, causes and effects are represented as coincident in space and time. We need have little hesitation in following Collingwood in denying the usefulness of this notion in history—or in other studies either, for that matter. In fact, as Collingwood more than half admits, it is a philosopher's invention; it is a bogus sense of the word 'thought to be' used in the theoretical sciences of nature. There is perhaps some excuse for the philosophers concerned in the fact that such sciences do enunciate simultaneity laws, and that, relative to some theory, and in the light of certain other conditions, it may be logically impossible for an effect not to follow a cause. But as Collingwood states Sense III, it is, as he says, self-contradictory.

In defining it as he does, however, Collingwood fails to prove the point he seems to want to make about the impro-

[1] Op. cit., p. 308.

priety of the causal concept outside the spheres of individual human relations and the practical sciences. For there is a perfectly proper use of 'cause' in the *applied* theoretical sciences. It is the sense brought to our attention by Ryle's doctrine of 'theory-loaded' causal terms. The sense in which a wound may be the cause of a scar is not included in Collingwood's threefold classification. In such a case, the relationship between cause and effect clearly falls short of the requirements of Sense III, while going beyond Sense II by virtue of the explanatory force of the causal assertion. Let us call this further use of the term 'Sense III*a*'. I call it this because it is the proper substitute for Collingwood's Sense III when we are applying theoretical science. It might, however, have been almost as appropriately designated Sense II*b*, since the requirement that there be a theoretical connexion between cause and effect would generally be applied *as well as*, and not instead of, Collingwood's criterion of the 'handle'. It seems to me that in his anxiety to discredit the metaphysically exaggerated Sense III, Collingwood overlooked this important 'scientific' sense of 'cause' altogether. And in doing so, although he would not have liked this suggestion, he failed to give a complete account of causal explanations in history either; for his classification leaves no room for the explanations historians may—perhaps only rarely—give in the light of theoretical knowledge derived from the social, or even the natural, sciences.

THE RATIONALE OF ACTIONS

1. *Historical Understanding as 'Empathetic'*

MY discussion of the covering law theory up to this point has been concerned chiefly with its applicability to explanations given of fairly large-scale historical events or conditions. I now want to direct attention to a narrower range of cases: the kind of explanation historians generally give of the *actions* of those individuals who are important enough to be mentioned in the course of historical narrative. It will be my thesis in this chapter that the explanation of individual human behaviour as it is usually given in history has features which make the covering law model peculiarly inept.

My argument in Chapter II was, in part, an attempt to clarify the sense in which historians' explanations can be, and often are, given of unique events: a doctrine commonly found in the writings of certain idealist philosophers of history. What I now wish to say may be regarded as an attempt to rehabilitate to some extent a second traditional doctrine of idealist philosophers of history which Gardiner has attacked at length: the view that the objects of historical study are fundamentally different from those, for example, of the natural sciences, because they are the actions of beings like ourselves; and that even if (for the sake of argument) we allow that natural events may be explained by subsuming them under empirical laws, it would still be true that this procedure is inappropriate in history. Sometimes such a view will be supported by the belief that human actions—at any rate the ones we call 'free'—do not fall under law at all. Sometimes it will be alleged only that even if they do fall under law, discovery of the law would still not enable us to understand them in the sense proper to this special subject-matter. It is the second of these claims which I especially want to consider here.

The doctrine is commonly expressed with the aid of a characteristic set of terms. To understand a human action, it will be said, it is necessary for the inquirer somehow to discover its 'thought-side'; it is not sufficient merely to know the pattern of overt behaviour. The historian must *penetrate* behind appearances, achieve *insight* into the situation, *identify* himself sympathetically with the protagonist, *project* himself imaginatively into his situation. He must *revive, re-enact, re-think, re-experience* the hopes, fears, plans, desires, views, intentions, &c., of those he seeks to understand. To explain action in terms of covering law would be to achieve, at most, an external kind of understanding. The historian, by the very nature of his self-imposed task, seeks to do more than this.

It is worth noticing that historians themselves, and not just professional philosophers of history, often describe their task in these terms. Professor Butterfield is representative of a large group of his professional colleagues when he insists that "the only understanding we ever reach in history is but a refinement, more or less subtle and sensitive, of the difficult—and sometimes deceptive—process of imagining oneself in another person's place". And elsewhere in *History and Human Relations*, he writes:

Our traditional historical writing . . . has refused to be satisfied with any merely causal or stand-offish attitude towards the personalities of the past. It does not treat them as mere things, or just measure such features of them as the scientist might measure; and it does not content itself with merely reporting about them in the way an external observer would do. It insists that the story cannot be told correctly unless we see the personalities from the inside, feeling with them as an actor might feel the part he is playing—thinking their thoughts over again and sitting in the position not of the observer but of the doer of the action. If it is argued that this is impossible—as indeed it is—not merely does it still remain the thing to aspire to, but in any case the historian must put himself in the place of the historical personage, must feel his predicament, must think as though he were that man. Without this art not only is it impossible to tell the story correctly but it is impossible to interpret the very documents on which the reconstruction depends. Traditional

historical writing emphasizes the importance of sympathetic imagination for the purpose of getting inside human beings. We may even say
that this is part of the science of history for it produces communi-
cable results—the insight of one historian may be ratified by scholars in
general, who then give currency to the interpretation that is produced....[1]

Among covering law logicians there is an 'official' answer
to philosophers or historians who talk in this way about the
peculiarities of 'historical understanding'. The answer is that
although there is something right about it, the element of truth
in such an account is not a point of logic; it is a mixture of
psychological description and methodological precept. As a
psychological description of the historian's state of mind when
he succeeds in explaining the action of one of his characters,
the notion of 'empathy' or 'imaginative understanding', as it
is often called, will be allowed some merit—although it will be
represented as involving us all too easily in the philosophical
error of thinking that merely having certain experiences, or
thinking certain thoughts similar to those of the historical
agents, itself constitutes understanding or explaining. Similarly, as a suggestion as to how to go about discovering what
the agent's motives were, the 'empathy' theory will be admitted
to have a certain methodological point—although the reserva-
tion will be made that the principle involved often leads the
investigator astray. Professor Hempel puts the position suc-
cinctly in the following passage:

The historian, we are told, imagines himself in the place of the persons involved in the events which he wants to explain; he tries to realize
as completely as possible the circumstances under which they acted, and
the motives which influenced their actions; and by this imaginary self-
identification with his heroes, he arrives at an understanding and thus
at an adequate explanation of the events with which he is concerned.

This method of empathy is, no doubt, frequently applied by laymen
and by experts in history. But it does not in itself constitute an explanation; it rather is essentially a heuristic device; its function is to suggest
certain psychological hypotheses which might serve as explanatory
principles in the case under consideration. Stated in crude terms, the
idea underlying this function is the following: the historian tries to
realize how he himself would act under the given conditions, and under

[1] pp. 145–6. See also pp. 116–17.

the particular motivations of his heroes; he tentatively generalizes his findings into a general rule and uses the latter as an explanatory principle in accounting for the actions of the persons involved. Now, this procedure may sometimes prove heuristically helpful; but its use does not guarantee the soundness of the historical explanation to which it leads. The latter rather depends upon the factual correctness of the empirical generalizations which the method of understanding may have suggested.

Nor is the use of this method indispensable for historical explanation. A historian may, for example, be incapable of feeling himself into the role of a paranoiac historic personality, and yet be able to explain certain of his actions; notably by reference to the principles of abnormal psychology. Thus whether the historian is or is not in a position to identify himself with his historical hero, is irrelevant for the correctness of his explanation; what counts, is the soundness of the general hypotheses involved, no matter whether they were suggested by empathy, or by a strictly behaviouristic procedure.[1]

Now I do not wish to deny that there is any value at all in this sort of objection. But I think it important to show that the argument does not cut as deeply as covering law theorists commonly assume. For in recognizing the mixture of psychological and methodological elements in many statements of the idealist position, and in denying that these amount to an analysis of logical structure, these theorists fail to notice what it is about explanations of human actions in history which make the idealists want to say what they do—albeit in a quasi-psychological and quasi-methodological way. And what is left out, I wish to maintain, should properly be taken into account in a *logical* analysis of explanation as it is given in history. I shall argue that idealist theory partially, and perhaps defectively, formulates a certain pragmatic criterion operating in explanations of action given by historians, and that when this is ignored, we are quite properly puzzled as to why certain alleged explanations, which meet the covering law requirements, would be dismissed by historians as unsatisfactory— perhaps even as 'no explanation at all'.

The discussion to follow may be regarded in part as an

[1] Op. cit., p. 467. A similar argument is used by Crawford, op. cit., p. 157; R. S. Peters, op. cit., p. 143; Gardiner, op. cit., p. 129; A. Danto, in 'Mere Chronicle and History Proper', *Journal of Philosophy*, 1953, p. 176.

attempt to 'make sense' of what Collingwood, in particular, has to say about historical understanding—and I make no apology for this. But although some reference will be made to dicta of his, I shall not offer any close textual discussion of his account. I shall try, rather, to bring out independently, by reference to examples, features which covering law theory seems to me to miss, going on thereafter to discuss likely misunderstandings of, and objections to, the logical point which appears to emerge out of such an examination.

2. Explaining and Justifying Actions

The following extract from G. M. Trevelyan's *The English Revolution* is typical of a wide range of explanations of individual actions to be found in ordinary historical writing. In the course of an account of the invasion of England by William of Orange, Trevelyan asks: "Why did Louis make the greatest mistake of his life in withdrawing military pressure from Holland in the summer of 1688?" His answer is:

He was vexed with James, who unwisely chose this moment of all, to refuse the help and advice of his French patron, upon whose friendship he had based his whole policy. But Louis was not entirely passion's slave. No doubt he felt irritation with James, but he also calculated that, even if William landed in England, there would be civil war and long troubles, as always in that factious island. Meanwhile, he could conquer Europe at leisure. "For twenty years," says Lord Acton, "it had been his desire to neutralize England by internal broils, and he was glad to have the Dutch out of the way (in England) while he dealt a blow at the Emperor Leopold (in Germany)." He thought "it was impossible that the conflict between James and William should not yield him an opportunity." This calculation was not as absurd as it looks after the event. It was only defeated by the unexpected solidity of a new type of Revolution.[1]

What Trevelyan here makes quite explicit is that, when we ask for the explanation of an action, what we very often want is a reconstruction of the agent's *calculation* of means to be adopted toward his chosen end in the light of the circumstances in which he found himself. To explain the action we need to know what considerations convinced him that he should act as he did.

[1] pp. 105–6.

But the notion of discovering the agent's calculation, it must be admitted, takes us no more than one preliminary step towards a satisfactory analysis of such explanations; and it may in itself be misleading. It must not be assumed, for instance, that the agent 'calculated' in the sense of deriving by strict deductive reasoning the practical conclusion he drew—i.e. that the various considerations are elements in a calculus. Indeed, Trevelyan's explanation provides an obvious example to the contrary. Nor should we assume that the explanatory calculation must have been recited in propositional form, either aloud or silently—a notion which one might be forgiven for extracting out of Collingwood's discussion of the way thought must be re-enacted by historians in order to understand intelligent, purposive actions. Not all high-grade actions are performed deliberately in the sense that they are undertaken with a plan consciously preformulated.

Indeed, it is tempting to say that in such cases there is *no* calculation to be *re*constructed by the historian. But such an admission need not affect the main point; for in so far as we say an action is purposive at all, no matter at what level of conscious deliberation, there is a calculation which could be constructed for it: the one the agent would have gone through if he had had time, if he had not seen what to do in a flash, if he had been called upon to account for what he did after the event, &c. And it is by eliciting some such calculation that we explain the action. It might be added that if the agent is to understand his *own* actions, i.e. after the event, he may have to do so by constructing a calculation in exactly the same way, although at the time he recited no propositions to himself. No doubt there are special dangers involved in such construction after the fact. But although we may have to examine very critically any particular example, the point is that when we do consider ourselves justified in accepting an explanation of an individual action, it will most often assume the general *form* of an agent's calculation.

Since the calculation gives what we should normally call the agent's *reasons* for acting as he did, I shall refer hereafter to this broad class of explanations as 'rational'. It should be clear that this use of the expression 'rational explanation' is a narrower one than is often found in philo-sophical and semi-philosophical literature. It is sometimes said, for instance, that all science, all systematic inquiry, seeks a rational explanation for what is observed, where all that is meant is an explanation which takes account of all the facts considered puzzling, and which does not violate, say, the canons of coherence and induction. I intend something much more restricted than this: an explanation which displays the *rationale* of what was done.

The goal of such explanation is to show that what was done was the thing to have done for the reasons given, rather than merely the thing that is done on such occasions, perhaps in accordance with certain laws (loose or otherwise). The phrase 'thing to have done' betrays a crucially important feature of explanations in terms of agent calculations—a feature quite different from any we have noticed so far. For the infinitive 'to do' here functions as a value term. I wish to claim therefore that there is an element of *appraisal* of what was done in such explanations; that what we want to know when we ask to have the action explained is in what way it was *appropriate*. In the ordinary course of affairs, a demand for explanation is often recognized to be at the same time a challenge to the agent to produce either justification or excuse for what was done. In history, too, I want to argue, it will often be found impossible to bring out the point of what is offered as explanation unless the overlapping of these notions, when it is human actions we are interested in, is explicitly recognized.

Once again, however, I must be on guard against overstat-ing the point; for I do not wish to imply that anything that is explained on the rational model is thereby certified *without qualification* as the right, or proper, or intelligent thing to have done. In saying that the explanation must exhibit what was done as appropriate or justified it is always necessary to add the philosopher's proviso: 'in a sense.'

The sense in question may be clarified if we note a scale

along which rational explanations can be ranged. The scale falls away from the simple case in which we can say: 'I find his action perfectly intelligible; he did exactly as I should have done.' It is a small step from such a case to one where we can understand an action when we see that it is what we should agree was the thing to do in view of the agent's peculiar circumstances. In such a case the explanation would consist of an account of these circumstances; they are the missing data which permit the construction of a calculation certifying the action as appropriate. Sometimes, of course, the agent is found to have been mistaken about the facts—including (as Trevelyan's example of Louis XIV shows) his views about what the results of certain lines of action will be. The agent is thus mistaken about the nature of his circumstances; yet his action can still be explained in the rational way so long as by bringing his erroneous beliefs to bear, the calculation can be satisfactorily constructed. It may also be necessary, at times, to take note explicitly of the agent's purposes, which may be quite different from the ones which the investigator would have had in the same circumstances, or even in the circumstances the agent envisaged. And the calculation may also have to take into account certain peculiar principles of the agent; for the action is rationally explained if it is in accordance with the agent's principles—no matter what we think of these.

There are thus gradations of rational explanation, depending on the amount of 'foreign' data which the investigator must bring in to complete the calculation: beliefs, purposes, principles, &c., of the agent which are different from those we might have assumed in absence of evidence to the contrary. Rational explanation may be regarded as an attempt to reach a kind of logical equilibrium at which point an action is *matched* with a calculation. A demand for explanation arises when the equilibrium is upset—when from the 'considerations' obvious to the investigator it is impossible to see the point of what was done. The function of the historian's explanatory story will in many cases be to sketch in the corrections to these 'obvious' considerations which require to be made if the reader is to be able to say: 'Now I understand what he was about.'[1]

In the light of this account, it should be clear how restricted is the sense in which a rational explanation, as I use the term here, must show that what was done was the appropriate or right thing to have done. It is not necessary for the historian to show that the agent had reason for what he did; it is sufficient for explanation to show that he had reasons. But the element of appraisal remains in that what the historian declares to have been the agent's reasons must really *be* reasons (from the agent's point of view). To record what the agent *said* his reasons were would not be enough to provide a rational explanation unless the cogency of such reported reasons could be appreciated by the historian, when any peculiar beliefs, purposes, or principles of the agent were taken into account. Reported reasons, if they are to be explanatory in the rational way, must be *good* reasons at least in the sense that *if* the situation had been as the agent envisaged it (whether or not we, from our point of vantage, concur in his view of it), then what was done would have been the thing to have done. The historian must be able to 'work' the agent's calculation.

3. *The Point of the 'Identification' Metaphor*

If my account of rational explanation is correct, what should we say about the view that historical understanding is 'empathetic'? It seems to me that our being able to range rational explanations along a scale in the way described above gives a real point to the 'projection' metaphors used by empathy theorists. Perhaps it is because the scale has been either ignored or misunderstood that what such theorists have said has been so easily written off as obvious but uninteresting, or as interesting but dangerous.

Covering law logicians commonly speak of empathy as a 'methodological dodge'. And it might, I suppose, be claimed that if an old, practised historian were to say to a novice: 'You will never understand the way medieval knights behaved

[1] See note C, p. 171.

unless you drop your 20th century prejudices and try to see things from their point of view', he *may* be telling the novice how to get on with his job, and thus be making a point which might be called 'methodological'. But I cannot believe that what the old hand offers his young colleague is (in Hempel's words) "a heuristic device" whose function is "to suggest certain psychological hypotheses which might serve as explanatory principles in the case under consideration". As Hempel goes on to explain, by this he means that the historian, since he lacks empirically tested psychological laws which fit, say, the behaviour of medieval knights, must do something about repairing the deficiency if he is ever to give an explanation of knightly activities; for according to the covering law theory there is no explanation without empirical laws. Clearly the historian, especially the novice, is in no position to work over the whole field himself in search of the required laws. So, according to Hempel, he takes a short cut; he imagines himself in the knight's position, asks himself what *he* would have done, generalizes the answer as an empirical law covering knights (i.e. from a single imaginary case), and in this way satisfies the logical requirements of the model.

Hempel warns us, of course, that the use of the 'device' does not "guarantee the soundness of the historical explanation to which it leads", which depends rather "upon the factual correctness of the empirical generalizations which the method of understanding may have suggested". That is, we may presume, further empirical confirmation of the generalization must come in before we can regard the explanation as anything more than an inspired guess. In Hempel's terminology, the generalization is only a "hypothesis" until it has received the sort of empirical confirmation and testing that any respectable scientific law must undergo, losing in the process the marks of its Athena-like origin.

In the light of what was said in the previous section, it should be clear how misleading this is as an account of 'empathetic understanding'. No doubt there *is* a methodological side to the doctrine; and it might be formulated in some such way as: 'Only by putting yourself in the agent's position can you *find out* why he did what he did.' Here the suggestion is admittedly that by an imaginative technique we shall discover some *new information*—the agent's motives or reasons for acting. When Collingwood says that historical understanding consists of penetrating to the thought-side of actions—discovering the thought and nothing further—the temptation to interpret this in the methodological way is understandably strong. But there is another way in which the doctrine can be formulated: 'Only by putting yourself in the agent's position can you *understand* why he did what he did.' The point of the 'projection' metaphor is, in this case, more plausibly interpreted as a logical one. Its function is not to remind us of *how we come to know* certain facts, but to formulate, however tentatively, certain *conditions which must be satisfied* before a historian is prepared to say: 'Now I have the explanation.'

To dismiss 'empathy' as a mere 'methodological dodge' is to assume, falsely, that all there is to notice when rational explanations are given is a second-rate method of obtaining the same sort of result as can be obtained more reliably by direct attempts to subsume what is to be explained under an empirical covering law. But, as I have tried to show, at least part of what is meant by talking about the 'need to project', &c., is not achievable at all by the method recommended by covering law theorists. To accept Hempel's argument against 'empathy' is to obliterate a distinction between explanation types: a distinction between representing something as the thing generally done, and representing it as the appropriate thing to have done. Thus, when Hempel, after the passage quoted, goes on to say: "The kind of understanding thus conveyed must be clearly separated from scientific understanding", I have no objection to make, provided that by 'scientific understanding' is meant 'knowing to fall under an empirical law'. But Hempel's account of the alternative is quite unsatisfactory. For 'empathetic understanding', interpreted as 'rational explanation', is *not* a matter of "presenting the pheno-

mena in question as somehow 'plausible' or 'natural' to us . . .
by means of attractively worded metaphors".

No doubt the widespread resistance to admitting the need
to cite anything more than antecedent conditions and a general
law in explaining actions owes something to the air of mystery
surrounding the language in which 'empathy' theory is often
framed: 'projection', 'identification', 'imagination', 'insight',
'intuition', &c. Such words arouse the suspicion that, if the
conditions of the covering law theory are not met, it will be
necessary to claim that the historian's explanation somehow
goes beyond the limits of empirical inquiry into the realm of
the unverifiable. As Gardiner puts it, historians often seem
to be credited with "an additional power of knowing which
allows them to 'penetrate into' the minds of the subjects of
their study and take, as it were, psychological X-ray photo-
graphs".[1] And in the bulletin of the American Social Science
Research Council already referred to, historians are warned
against a view of 'historical understanding' supposed to be
"achieved not by introducing general laws or relevant antecedent events, but by an act of 'intuition', 'imaginative identification', 'empathy' or 'valuation' which makes the historical
occurrence plausible or intelligible", and whose adequacy is
determined by "a self-certifying insight".[2] To allow the legitimacy of empathy appears to many of its opponents as the
granting of a licence to eke out scanty evidence with imaginative filler.

It is therefore worth my denying explicitly that what I have
called rational explanation is in any damaging sense beyond
empirical inquiry. As I have pointed out already, it has an
inductive, empirical side, for we build up to explanatory
equilibrium *from the evidence*. To get inside Disraeli's shoes
the historian does not simply ask himself: 'What would I have
done?'; he reads Disraeli's dispatches, his letters, his speeches,
&c.—and not with the purpose of discovering antecedent conditions falling under some empirically validated law, but rather
in the hope of appreciating the problem as Disraeli saw it. The

---

[1] Op. cit., p. 128.   [2] *Bulletin No. 54*, p. 128.

attempt to provide rational explanation is thus—if you like the term—'scientific' explanation in a broad sense; there is no question of the investigator letting his imagination run riot. Indeed, many 'empathy' theorists have expressly guarded against such a misinterpretation of their views. To Butterfield, for instance, historical understanding is not a deliberate commission of the sin of anachronism; it is a "process of emptying oneself in order to catch the outlook and feelings of men not like-minded with oneself".[1]

It is true, of course, that the *direction* of inquiry in the explanation of actions is generally from what the inquirer presumes the relevant agent calculation to be—using his own, or his society's conception of rational purposes and principles —to what he discovers to be the peculiar data of the historical agent: a direction suggested by the scale already indicated. In view of this, Butterfield's admonition to 'empty ourselves' is a little sweeping. In achieving rational explanation of an action we do project—but we project from our own point of view. In each case, the inclusion of 'foreign' data in the calculation requires positive evidence that the agent was *not* like-minded with us. The historian does not build up to explanatory equilibrium from scratch. But this is far from admitting the covering law objection that the whole direction of the inquiry amounts to a vicious methodology. The procedure is self-corrective.

There is thus no reason to think that what I am calling 'rational' explanations are put forward as self-evidently true, as some philosophers who talk of 'insight' may seem to imply. Collingwood has sometimes been thought to provide justification for those who attack empathy theory on this account —e.g. when he represents the understanding of an action as an immediate leap to the discovery of its 'inside', without the aid of any general laws, and (it may appear) without the use of any inductive reasoning at all.[2] But it is always possible that a

[1] Op. cit., p. 146.
[2] e.g. "When [the historian] knows what happened, he already knows why it happened" (*The Idea of History*, p. 214).

mistake has been made in the inductive reasoning which provided the factual information for the calculation. It is always
possible that further data may come in which will upset the
logical equilibrium—perhaps evidence that the agent did not
know something which it was at first thought he did. The
ability of the historian to go through what he takes to be a
relevant calculation does not guarantee the correctness of the
explanation given; correct *form* is never a guarantee of correct
content. But this is nothing more than the normal hazard of
any empirical inquiry.

4. *Generalizations and Principles of Action*

Some exponents of the covering law model, while accepting
the thesis of the two preceding sections, may object that this
only amounts to recognizing an additional condition of a pragmatic sort which explanations must often satisfy in ordinary
historical writing. It may be held, therefore, that what I say
about rational explanation affects the claims of covering law
theory only on its sufficient condition side. It seems to me,
however, that in cases where we want to elicit the rationale of
what was done, there are special reasons for regarding the
model as false or misleading on its necessary condition side
as well. For in an important sense, rational explanation falls
short of, as well as goes beyond, subsuming a case under a
general empirical law.

Any argument to the effect that a satisfactory or complete
rational explanation must subsume what is explained under
an empirically ascertainable 'regularity' depends on treating
the data of the agent's calculation as 'antecedent conditions'
(no doubt a very complicated set). It will be said that no
matter what *else* is said about these conditions, they must be
data from which what was done could have been predicted;
and that the only difficulties we should encounter in trying
to formulate the implicit covering law linking these to actions
of the kind performed would be the ones discussed in Chapter
II above (which I propose to ignore here). If we say: 'Disraeli
attacked Peel because Peel was ruining the landed class', we

mean *inter alia* that anyone like Disraeli in certain respects would have done the same thing in a situation similar in certain respects—the respects in question being discovered by pressing for amplification of the single reason given.

Now this objection is an important one, because its plausibility arises out of a genuine characteristic of rational explanation which ought to be made clear. For it is quite true that 'reasons for acting' as well as 'conditions for predicting' have a kind of generality or universality. If y is a good reason for A to do x, then y would be a good reason for anyone sufficiently like A to do x under sufficiently similar circumstances. But this universality of reasons is unlike the generality of an empirically validated law in a way which makes it especially hazardous to say that by giving a rational explanation, an historian commits himself to the truth of a corresponding law. For if a negative instance is found for a general empirical law, the law itself must be modified or rejected, since it states that people *do* behave in a certain way under certain circumstances. But if a negative instance is found for the sort of general statement which might be extracted out of a rational explanation, the latter would not necessarily be falsified. For that statement would express a judgement of the form: 'When in a situation of type $C_1 \ldots C_n$ the thing to do is x.' The 'implicit law' in such explanation is better called a *principle of action* than a generalization (or even a principle of inference).[1]

It is true that finding a large number of negative instances —finding that people often do not act in accordance with it— would create a presumption against the claim of a given principle to universal validity. But it would not *compel* its withdrawal; and if it was not withdrawn, the explanatory value of the principle for those actions which *were* in accordance with it would remain. It is true, too, that if a particular person often acted at variance with a principle which he was said to hold, the statement that he held that principle would come into question. But that statement would not *necessarily* be falsified; and if it were retained, we could still explain in the

---

[1] See Note D, p. 171.

rational way those of his actions which *were* in accordance with it. The connexion between a principle of action and the 'cases' falling under it is thus intentionally and peculiarly loose.

I do not deny, of course, that we often *can* predict successfully a person's response to a situation if we know, among other things, what his principles are (in so far as they are peculiar). In representing the action as the thing to have done, even in the extended sense required for rational explanation, we to some extent license the conclusion that it was the thing to have expected. Having said '*A* did *x* because of *y*', where *y* is *A*'s reason for doing *x*, we could also say that a bystander who knew the fact *y*, and also knew what *A*'s purposes and principles were, should not be surprised at *A*'s doing *x*. It is thus easy enough, under the guidance of a general theory of explanation which requires it, to slip into believing that the real force of the original explanation resides in alleviating such surprise; that its point is to show that this is the kind of thing we can expect to be done by such a person in such circumstances, and that the justification for the expectation must be found in experience of similar cases.

The widespread failure to distinguish between explanations which 'apply' empirical laws and those which 'apply' principles of action may owe something to the fact that the word 'because' is systematically ambiguous in this connexion. Taken in isolation, it is very seldom beyond all doubt whether a given explanatory statement of the form 'He did *x* because of *y*' is to be taken in the rational sense or not, i.e. whether the 'because' derives its explanatory force from an empirical law or a principle. The particular 'because' does not carry its language level on its face; this has to be determined by other means. It is thus often possible to interpret an explanation at the wrong level for a long time without committing any obvious logical errors. And this leaves plenty of room for manœuvring by philosophers who have a thesis to maintain which requires that only one level be recognized.

Whether an explanation of a piece of behaviour is to be

interpreted rationally or not will often depend on the context of utterance; we may have to ask how the explanation would be argued for, what else would be said if it were expanded, &c. Take the following example from Trevelyan's discussion of the problem of the early eighteenth-century smog in London:

> On days when the north-east wind carried the smoke-cloud, even Chelsea became dangerous to the asthmatic, as the mild philosopher Earl of Shaftesbury had reason to complain. There is no wonder that King William with his weak lungs had lived at Hampton Court when he could, and at Kensington when he must.[1]

The explanation offered can easily be reduced to a 'because' statement. But what exactly does the historian mean to imply: does he mean that any person *would* have done so, circumstances being what they were? Or does he mean that any *sensible* person would have done so? The explanation could surely be pushed either way, depending on how we cared to read it. And the explanation may be satisfactory (in the sense of 'adequate for its type') no matter which way it is read. Butterfield would no doubt elect to defend it in the second, or rational, way, while Gardiner, in the interests of his thesis, could choose the regularity way without obvious logical error. We cannot settle the issue between them until the writer gives us a more definite indication of what he intends. It is worth noticing, in this connexion, that many of the examples used by Gardiner to support the covering law model could be plausibly re-analysed in the rational way. The force of the explanation of Louis XIV's unpopularity in terms of his policies being detrimental to French interests is very likely to be found in the detailed description of the aspirations, beliefs, and problems of Louis's subjects. Given these men and their situation, Louis and his policies, their dislike of the king was an *appropriate* response.

Nor is the ambiguity confined to the word 'because'; it can be traced through a wide variety of terms used to describe and explain actions. It can be found, for instance, in the terms 'natural' and 'humanly possible', which Mr. W. H. Walsh

---

[1] *English Social History*, London, 1946, p. 337.

employs in *An Introduction to Philosophy of History*, when arguing that explanations of action in history are accomplished by means of basic non-technical generalizations.[1] "We are agreed", Walsh declares, "that to understand an historical situation we must bring some kind of general knowledge to bear on it, and the first question to ask here is clearly in what this general knowledge consists." Against the positivists he maintains that the most important generalizations used in an historian's explanations do not come from any of the sciences; they are fundamental judgements about human nature— "judgments about the characteristic responses human beings made to the various challenges set them in the course of their lives, whether by the natural conditions in which they live, or by their fellow beings". These constitute a 'science of human nature' distinguishable from scientific psychology; they provide the historian with a criterion of what is 'humanly possible', when he seeks to understand the past.

But the 'science of human nature' here described does not differ logically from scientific psychology; it is really just the common-sense psychology of the plain man. If left at that, Walsh's argument would make no other point against the positivists than Hempel's own admission that, because of the unfortunate backwardness of the science of psychology, historians must formulate many of the 'laws of human nature' required on the basis of their own experience. But the facts of historical writing which stimulate Walsh's sympathy with the idealists seem to me to require our drawing, not a distinction merely between different *sources* of empirical laws used, but between different *types* of explanation. For we sometimes want to explain actions not by representing them as instances of laws, but as the reasonable thing to have done; and when we do, if we appeal to 'general knowledge' at all, it is to principles of behaviour rather than empirical generalizations; to knowledge of what to do rather than of what is usually or always done.

Walsh does not put it this way, yet there are suggestions of

[1] Chap. III, sections 4, 5.

the point in some of his remarks. For instance, in pointing out that the basic general knowledge which historians bring to their work differs from one historian to another, he includes both knowledge of how men *do* and (he adds 'perhaps') *should* behave.[1] And again, in a footnote, he considers favourably Ryle's term 'knowledge how' (i.e. practical knowledge of some kind) as a characterization of what is to be included in the envisaged 'science of human nature'.[2] There is a hint of the same view in his acceptance of the suggestion that the 'science' in question is continuous with common sense—which, it may be remarked, is generally taken to cover our knowledge of what to do, as well as of what is generally done.[3] And the use of 'challenge-response' terminology in describing the nature of the fundamental judgements concerned points roughly in the same direction.[4]

Walsh's terms 'humanly possible' and 'human nature' are located at the centre of the difficulty; they straddle the distinction between explanation types, or between the levels of language at which we talk about actions. Consider the following explanatory remark of Ramsey Muir about a political decision of George III. "The king", he writes, ". . . naturally chose Shelburne rather than the hated Whigs."[5] In a way, this word does, as Walsh might say, represent the action as a characteristic response, in that anyone with George III's political memories would have tried to keep the Whigs out. But there is a very strong suggestion, too, that this response was *appropriate* in a rational sense; to say the choice naturally went to Shelburne is to imply that this was obviously the right thing for the king to do—from his point of view. Similarly, saying that an historian has a keen appreciation of what is 'humanly possible' *may* refer to the sort of law-governed phenomenon Walsh cites, e.g. "that men who undergo great physical privations are for the most part lacking in mental energy". But I think it may just as well refer to the fundamental

[1] p. 69. [2] p. 67.
[3] p. 66. [4] p. 65.
[5] *A Short History of the British Commonwealth*, vol. ii, p. 105.

principles on which any man may be expected to order his activities.

5. *The Standpoint of Historical Writing*

I have argued that rational explanation is a recognizably distinct type of explanation; that it employs a criterion of intelligibility which is different from that formulated by the covering law model, and that there are special reasons for objecting to the claim that such explanations require the truth of corresponding empirical laws. Let me now ask what we can say about the relation between such explanation and other kinds, and what, in general, is its role in historical writing.

It seems to me that there is a general presumption that a given action will be explicable on the rational model if we study it closely enough. The general belief that people act for sufficient reason does not arise out of definite pieces of evidence in particular cases; it is a *standing* presumption which requires contrary evidence in a particular case to defeat. Acknowledging the presumption does not imply that all actions must ultimately be done for sufficient reasons—even in the weak sense sketched in the foregoing sections; but it does register the conviction that it will generally be worth while making a sustained effort to 'save the appearances' rationally. If the first calculation we try to match with an action fails to fit it, then we normally consider ourselves obliged to look for evidence of additional, and perhaps queer, beliefs, &c., of the agent which, when explicitly recognized, permit the construction of a calculation which enjoins what was done. On the other hand, if we have satisfactorily achieved an equilibrium, we tend to regard this as a proper stopping place. The rational explanation of an action at a particular level carries a certain degree of plausibility on its face.

It is impossible to set theoretical limits to the guiding force of the presumption of rationality. It may often, for instance, lead us into attributing unconscious motives for action. Psychoanalysts seem to find it therapeutically useful to extend the scope of the presumption beyond the limits which would be countenanced in ordinary historical writing. But although no firm boundary can be drawn here, it is nevertheless necessary to recognize the fact that there will be particular cases in which we find it impossible to rationalize what was done, so that if an explanation is to be given at all, it will have to be of another kind. To say *a priori* that all actions must have a rationale, no matter how hard to discover, is just a dogma—although we could make it analytically true by a suitable definition of 'action'. In the ordinary course of affairs, rational and non-rational explanations of actions are alternatives—and alternatives sought in a certain order. We give reasons if we can, and turn to empirical laws if we must.[1]

Not only is this done in the ordinary course of affairs; it is done, too, in ordinary historical writing. Historians, as well as plain men, tend to push their explanations as high up the 'scale of understanding' as possible. Proof for this assertion would have to rest upon a detailed examination of historical writing, which cannot be undertaken here. But the following quotation appears to me typical in what it reveals about the workaday approach of historians to the problem of explaining human actions. In *The English Revolution*, while describing the last years of the Interregnum, I. D. Jones remarks:

It would be falsifying history to bring order out of the confusion of the year between the fall of Richard and the return of Charles II. *There is no logic or reason in it.* The resurrections and re-burials of the Rump: the meteoric energies and extinction of Lambert, now a Fifth Monarchist, now considered an eligible father-in-law to Charles Stuart: *the cryptic evolution of Monck* from the Cromwellian, Republican, Presbyterian to Royalist: the alliances of Fleetwood with Ludlow, Lambert, the Anabaptists and the Rump—all these events produce a tangled skein of desperation, irresolution and treachery *which needs a psychologist's rather than a historian's analysis.*[2]

The passage suggests that Jones has an ideal of explanation which he finds frustratingly inapplicable to the case of, for example, Monck's observed behaviour in 1658-9. He is so

---

[1] The relation between giving the reasons for, and giving the causes of, an action is a little more complicated. I discuss this in section 7.

[2] London, 1931, p. 106, my italics.

accustomed to using it in the course of his work that he appropriates it as *the* model of 'historical explanation', relegating the other kind (like Collingwood) to the attention of psychologists.[1] In so sharply repudiating any responsibility for giving a psychological explanation, Jones no doubt goes too far; for if a psychological theory were necessary and available to explain Monck's 'cryptic' behaviour, it would be the historian's business to use it, and it would be of interest to the reader to know it. But except in history deliberately written to a thesis, non-rational explanation only supplements, it does not replace, the rational sort.

In this respect history is logically continuous with literature rather than social science, if by the latter we mean something like a social 'physics'. This sort of claim has often been made, but usually for reasons which fail to reduce the cogency of the covering law theory as an account of the logical structure of all explanation. Trevelyan, for instance, seems to regard the use of narrative in the presentation of results as the feature which puts history among the humanities.[2] For to a narrative exposition, the canons of literary taste apply. The authors of the American Social Science Research Council's *Bulletin No. 64*, on the other hand, regard much historical writing as "in the tradition of the humanities" because, on their view, its conclusions lack empirical verification.[3] Both views leave the logical claims of the model intact. But my claim is rather that certain criteria of *what shall count as explanation* are applied throughout the humane studies which have, to say the least, a doubtful place in most programmes of social science. Even those who deplore this fact have often seen the point at issue. F. J. Teggart, a self-conscious reformer of history, in attacking the unregenerate kind, observes sourly: "The intelligibility which the historian thus introduces into the materials which he selects for his composition is of the same order as that pro-

---

[1] In *The Idea of History* (p. 29) Collingwood attacks history whose "chief purpose is to affirm laws, psychological laws". This, he says, is "not history at all, but natural science of a special kind".

[2] *History and the Reader*, London, 1945, pp. 10 ff.; and Trevelyan's plea for 'literary history' in *Clio, A Muse*, London, 1930, pp. 140–76.   [3] pp. 130–1.

vided by the author of a historical novel or drama."[1] The comparison is, of course, in Teggart's eyes quite damning.

What is at stake here is the proper 'standpoint' or 'approach' to at any rate a large part of the subject-matter of history. Collingwood declares that history is not a *spectacle*.[2] What he means could perhaps be put in terms of a distinction between two standpoints from which human actions can be studied. When we subsume an action under a law, our approach is that of a spectator of the action; we look for a pattern or regularity in it. But when we give an explanation in terms of the purpose which guided the action, the problem which it was intended to resolve, the principle which it applied, &c., we adopt the standpoint from which the action was done: the standpoint of an agent. In adopting this standpoint, the investigator appreciates the agent's problem and appraises his response to it. The importance in history of explanations given from the agent's standpoint gives some point to well-known idealist dicta like 'All history is contemporary history', and 'All history is history of thought'. Such slogans are exaggerated and paradoxical, but they do register an awareness that the problems of historical agents have to be faced by the reader and the investigator if they are to understand what was done.

It should, perhaps, be added that the historian's preference for the rational model sometimes leads him into making highly elliptical explanatory statements when group rather than individual behaviour is being considered—statements which have sometimes scandalized literal-minded philosophers when they have come to analyse them. In highly condensed general histories, classes and nations and societies are often personified and written about in a quasi-rational way. Thus Germany's attack on Russia in 1941 may be explained by citing the threat of Russian encirclement—as if a 'calculation' of this sort were relevant to the actions of a super-agent called 'Germany'. The precise analysis of such statements would, no doubt, often present difficulties; but I think it is clear that reference to the

---

[1] *Theory and Processes of History*, Berkeley and Los Angeles, 1941, p. 78.
[2] Op. cit., pp. 164, 214.

more detailed studies on which such general histories rest would show that what the 'calculation' in question really explains is the actions of those individuals who were authorized to act 'for Germany'. In other cases the actions of groups are explained on the rational model by means of a kind of 'typical' calculation—e.g. when an historian asks why the Puritans, in particular, became exercised about taxation in seventeenth-century England, or why the Slavs were especially hostile to the Hapsburg monarchy in the early years of the present century. Such extensions of rational explanation would appear to raise no problem other than the practical one of determining whether, in a particular case, the group concerned is homogeneous enough for this kind of treatment.

A different, although related, problem which is sometimes raised by the extension of what I have called rational explanation beyond the sphere of particular actions of particular individuals, is whether the motives, purposes, circumstances, &c., of historical agents afford *sufficient* explanation of large-scale historical phenomena. There is, as Whitehead has put it, a "senseless side" to history;[1] and by this he means more than that natural phenomena, which cannot, of course, be explained rationally, have to be taken into account by historians. For the 'senseless' also appears in larger-scale social results of individual actions which are not themselves explicable on the rational model because they are not what any individual— even one acting for a group—intended or even wanted to happen; and they may often, indeed, be quite the reverse. According to Mrs. K. Cornforth, it is precisely this sort of thing (e.g. "the introduction of steam in modern times, and the development of the cinema industry") which can be explained by general 'scientific' theories of the historical process; and she regards such explanations as the more profound and important ones.[2] M. R. Cohen, too, warns us against

---

[1] *Adventures of Ideas*, Cambridge, 1933, p. 8.
[2] 'Explanation in History', *Proceedings of the Aristotelian Society, Supp. Vol.*, 1935, p. 137.

exaggerating the extent to which the notion of 'purpose' can be appealed to in explaining social phenomena.[1] The voyage of Columbus was a cause of the spread of European civilization to America, but the result is not explained by the voyage, nor did Columbus intend it.

What Cornforth and Cohen say has a certain point, but it can be misleading. For to say that the sort of phenomena they have in mind cannot be explained, or explained adequately, in purposive terms may mean one or another of two things. If it means merely that they cannot be explained in terms of the purposes of some individual who stage-managed the whole thing, then of course no objection need be raised at all. But if they mean that a perfectly adequate explanation of the gross event cannot be given in terms of the rationale of the activities of the various individuals involved—and this is strongly suggested—then it is surely necessary to disagree. An historian's explanation of the spread of European civilization to America will normally be what I called in Chapter II 'piecemeal'; and it will involve a detailed examination, mainly in rational terms, of the activities and motives of countless individuals and groups; the French Jesuits and the English Puritans as well as Columbus; Colbert and Raleigh as well as Philip II; fur traders, explorers, gold-seekers, land-hungry peasants, and a host of others. As for the question whether explanation can or cannot, should or should not, be given in terms of 'theories of the historical process' where these are available, all that needs to be said is that this would be uncharacteristic of ordinary historical writing. And I can see no reason to brand the more characteristic sort of thing less 'profound'.

6. *The Model of the Dispositional Statement*

There remains the question of how my account of typical explanations of action in history squares with the alternative analysis offered by Gardiner in *The Nature of Historical Explanation*. Gardiner's account of the way we are "to interpret

---

[1] 'The Social Sciences and the Natural Sciences', *The Social Sciences and their Interrelations*, eds. W. F. Ogburn and A. Goldenweiser, Boston, 1927, pp. 445–6.

explanations in terms of motives, desires, intentions, and so forth" is summarized in the following passage, with reference to the example: 'John hit you with a hammer because he is bad-tempered.' Of this statement, he writes:

It would be absurd to deny that this is an explanation: but it would be equally ludicrous to imagine that it could in some manner be 'reduced' to an explanation asserting a causal relation between two events or processes, one of which is labelled 'John's bad temper'. 'John is bad-tempered' is a sentence which, amongst other things, is predictive of how John is likely to behave in various (only vaguely indicated) types of situations. The function of the 'because' in the statement alluded to is to set a statement referring to a specific action within the context of a general statement about John's behaviour which can be 'unpacked' into an indefinite range of statements concerning his reactions to various kinds of circumstances. It represents, if you like, an *instance* of how he can in general be expected to behave under certain conditions. It sets John's action within a pattern, the pattern of his normal behaviour.

It is in terms of this usage of 'explanation', rather than in terms of the cause-effect usage, that historians' (and ordinary persons') accounts of human actions of the kind we are considering are to be understood. This is not to say that it would be correct to bundle together into an amorphous heap historical explanations referring to desires, intentions, purposes, plans, and programmes, as if there were not important differences between them. To say that an individual's actions were planned or conformed to a programme or policy may be very different from saying that they were intended; and again, to say that they were intended can be different from saying that they were motivated by such-and-such a desire. And these cases again are different from those in which we say that his actions were 'reasoned' or 'considered'. But in all these instances it is with explanation in the sense of fitting a particular action within a certain pattern that we are concerned. The patterns are familiar to us both from experience of our own behaviour and from experience of the ways other people behave; and it is in virtue of this that we are able to make the inferences and provide the explanations in question.[1]

Gardiner here contends that statements attributing motives, purposes, intentions, &c., have a peculiar and complex logical form. He admits that such statements cannot be forced into the Procrustean Bed of the covering law model, and in admitting this, he parts company with both Popper and Hempel.

[1] pp. 124-5.

In a passage quoted in Chapter I, Popper remarks: "... if we explain Caesar's decision to cross the Rubicon by his ambition and energy, say, then we are using some very trivial psychological generalizations which would hardly ever arouse the attention of a psychologist". And Hempel, too, goes out of his way to deny that explanations in terms of the motives of individuals raise any difficulties for the covering law analysis. Such explanations, he says, are not "essentially different from the causal explanations of physics and chemistry". For Hempel, motives are antecedent conditions which must be linked to resulting actions by covering laws before they have explanatory force.[1] Presumably he would deal in a similar way with all those explanations which attribute desires, emotions, purposes, plans, &c., to historical agents.

Gardiner's refusal to follow Popper and Hempel here is based on a general analysis of 'mental conduct concepts' similar to the one offered by Ryle in *The Concept of Mind*.[2] According to Ryle, laws connect events or govern processes—but motives are neither events nor processes. The notion that a motive could be a special kind of antecedent condition or cause of actions, i.e. a mental kind, he repudiates as a 'logical howler'; for if true, it would make a large range of causal statements about actions empirically unverifiable—not just in practice, but in principle. It is not just that, in the case of other people, we cannot observe the ghostly events or processes—the various motives—which would have to be mentioned in the protases of the law statements supposed to be required for causal explanation. We cannot properly be said to observe such mental causes even in ourselves—a contention which undercuts any protest that we argue by analogy from our own experience to the existence of mental causes correlated with other people's overt behaviour. Ryle maintains that our ordinary use of motive language lends support to his thesis here. To put it formally: if motive words name events

---

[1] Such laws, linking motive with action motivated, should not be confused with laws linking circumstances with actions responding to them.
[2] London, 1949, especially chap. iv.

or processes, then event-predicates and process-predicates should be applicable. But, as Ryle's book is designed to show in impressive detail, the attempt to apply them generates nonsense.

If, for these reasons, explanation in terms of motives cannot require the currency of a general law, what is its logical force? Ryle answers this question with a general account of the logic of dispositional characteristics. He argues that to attribute a motive to an agent is to relate the motivated action to certain other things the agent did, or would have done, in these and other circumstances. To use Gardiner's phrase, the "function of the 'because' " in a motive explanation is to indicate the general pattern of behaviour of which the particular action is a part. The logical model for explanation of this kind is given at its simplest in Ryle's celebrated contrast between two kinds of thing we can say about the breaking of a pane of glass. If we say 'The glass broke when the stone hit it because whenever stones hit glass it breaks', we give (subject to the qualifications urged in preceding chapters) a law-covered explanation. But if we say 'The glass broke when the stone hit it because it is brittle', we explain what happened in terms of a dispositional property of glass. The dispositional characteristic 'being brittle' is neither an additional antecedent happening nor a law. It has, however, an explanatory value of its own because, like a law, there is generality in it.

A statement attributing a dispositional characteristic like 'brittle' might be called 'lawlike' because, like a law, it is at least partly hypothetical in what it implies; it can be satisfied by a wide range of behaviour, of which shattering on the impact of a stone is only one kind. The relation which covering law theorists claim to find between prediction and explanation is therefore, to some extent, preserved. If we know that glass is brittle, we know what sort of thing to expect when we hear that a brick has been thrown at a window pane. The precision of prediction decreases, of course, with the complexity of the behaviour pattern indicated by the dispositional term. In the case of glass, and in the case of human reflexes and

habits—Ryle's 'single-track' or determinate dispositions—
actualizations follow a narrowly restricted pattern. But in the
case of motives—which are 'many-tracked' or determinable—
they do not. Thus to say that Disraeli attacked Peel in 1846
because he was ambitious is to imply only that the attack was
one of a number of things, systematically related, which the
use of the word 'ambition' licenses us to expect. It is not to
imply that from the conditions of 1846 it could have been
deduced (with the aid of the dispositional statement) that he
would make such an attack.

Covering law theorists may be tempted to argue that the
connexion between dispositional and law-covered explanations is really much closer than I have made it appear; for
just as, in the case of the breaking glass, we may assume that
the dispositional property holds by virtue of certain physical
laws concerning the behaviour of glass and bricks, so the dispositional properties attributed to human agents may appear
to be applicable because of there being regularities in human
behaviour which are formulable in terms of laws (however
'loose'). But if this is taken to mean that a dispositional
explanation of a particular human action depends in any way
on the truth of such laws, it involves a misunderstanding of
the distinction which has been drawn between explanation
types. For 'ambition' is not a *general* characteristic of men
(or even, perhaps, of politicians) in the way 'being brittle' is of
glass. To say 'Disraeli attacked Peel because he was ambitious'
draws attention to the general pattern of action into which his
particular action fits, but it implies nothing about the kind of
men from whom this kind of action can be expected. It merely
implies that action of this general pattern can be expected
from Disraeli; it subsumes his action under a regularity said to
hold for a particular person, rather than a regularity said to
hold for all persons of a certain type.[1] Dispositional explanation thus falls short of law-covered explanation in its *particularity* (a point which Gardiner's brief discussion may not
have made clear). It is accidental, not essential, to the explana-

[1] See Note E, p. 171.

tion, that in the case of the glass we know that objects of this *kind* will have the dispositional property mentioned. The modification of the covering law theory represented by the recognition of dispositional explanation is therefore quite a major one.

Like explanations in terms of a covering generalization, dispositional explanations often appear so trivial as to invite the judgement: 'Really no explanation at all.' In general, the more 'single-track' the disposition referred to, the more trivial will the explanation appear. This helps to explain the fact that the logical respectability of dispositional explanation has not always been admitted even in quarters where 'regularity' is taken as the watchword. Crawford, for instance, attacks his fellow historian, Lord Elton, in withering terms for declaring, in an account of the failure of local government in the early years of the French Revolution: "Centralization is in the blood of Frenchmen; and Frenchmen must be administered, even if they are not governed." This Crawford castigates as a mere "seeming explanation".[1] It can be reduced, he says, to the statement: "Frenchmen preferred centralized administration because they had the habit of preferring centralized administration." And this (although formally sound on the dispositional model) he finds quite unenlightening. Crawford's 'reduction' of this rather flowery example of dispositional explanation to a 'habit' statement may perhaps go too far. But any answer to the question 'Why?' which *could* be reduced to 'It's habitual with him', would at least leave room for argument as to whether it offered a very trivial explanation, or avoided the demand for explanation altogether.

The majority of dispositional statements about people, however, are not trivial in this way, and it is not hard to discover historical examples whose logical force is much more plausibly elicited by Ryle's model of the breaking glass than by the original covering law theory. S. R. Gardiner, for instance, explains the fatal policy of Charles I dispositionally when he observes: "What he was doing he did from a *love of order*,

[1] Op. cit., p. 16.

combined with sheer *ignorance* of mankind." And the same sort of explanation is often also given of the behaviour of groups, for example, in accounting for the peculiarities of Irish Americans by referring to their Anglophobia.

The question which remains to be answered, however, is whether *all* explanations of human action in terms of motives, intentions, purposes, &c., can be accounted for in terms of the dispositional model: in particular, whether dispositional analysis brings out the real point of what, in previous sections, I called 'rational explanation'. And it seems to me clear enough that it does not. A pure dispositional explanation tells us that the person or thing under investigation tended to do things of (perhaps roughly) the sort done, under certain (unspecified) circumstances. It shows that what was done was the sort of thing we might have expected—it was the sort of thing that *would be* done by this person or thing. But in most historical contexts, such an explanation would tell us scarcely anything we really wanted to know when we asked: 'Why did he do it?' For in giving the dispositional answer, the *point* of what was done tends to drop out of sight. To attempt to analyse explanations of the form, '*A* did *x* in order to achieve *y*', as covertly dispositional simply ignores the question which we may reasonably assume the investigator to have had in mind when he represented this *as* an explanation.

It is not without significance in this connexion to remark that dispositional explanation is very frequently given in history where it is necessary to head off the reader's incipient demand to know 'Why?' in the rational sense. The following example of a genuine dispositional explanation of a rather complex sort illustrates the point. I. D. Jones, in accounting for Cromwell's political decisions of the late 1640's, declares:

His speeches and letters show his difficulty in reaching decisions and his reluctance to assume responsibility; he had not the mind that could plan ahead, but the genius that acted on impulse. He originated none of the many schemes of his party; he took fire from the ideas of others, such as Ireton, Harrison and Lambert. He waited, often in agonies of indecision, for guidance from "Providences"—the hand of God revealed in events; he read the omens like a Roman Consul. This, alone and adequately, explains his sudden adoption of the extremists in May 1647 and December 1648, and his final decision on Charles' death. . . . [1]

Here Jones explains the impulsive, inadequately reasoned decisions of 1647–8 by locating them in a general pattern of Cromwell's behaviour during those years. When we see them in this context of dispositions we are no longer surprised. Similarly, in the case of the explanation of the policy of Charles I, quoted above, the historian—perhaps because of the great stupidity of the king's behaviour—is content to show that it was characteristic.

But although dispositional characterization may alleviate surprise, it does not do it by revealing the point or rationale of what was done. For 'disposition' is a spectator's word; it belongs to the language of observing and predicting, rather than of deliberating and deciding. If the *agent* were to explain his action by pointing out which of his dispositional characteristics he had actualized, his explanation would seem oddly irrelevant. Nor should we think of saying: 'So that's the disposition Smith was actualizing! Now I see what he was up to!' It is true, of course, that many of the component factual statements of a rational explanation—e.g. statements of what the agent's beliefs and attitudes were—may be accepted on the basis of arguments of the form: 'He tends to do so-and-so, so he must believe so-and-so.' And it may even be alleged that belief is, itself, a dispositional characteristic. But to allow this would not be to admit that the explanation given by means of such factual statements is itself dispositional in form.

In his discussion of dispositional analysis, Ryle warns us that we must avoid "equating understanding with psychological diagnosis, i.e. with causal inferences from overt behaviour to mental processes in accordance with laws yet to be discovered by the psychologists . . .".[2] With this I have no quarrel, but I think the statement just as true if 'psychological diagnosis' is taken more broadly than Ryle's proviso allows. For we must also avoid equating understanding with merely

[1] *The English Revolution*, p. 85.   [2] Op. cit., p. 58.

recognizing that actions fall under certain behaviour patterns, or that they are likely to be preceded and followed by actions of a related kind.

In saying this I am not complaining, as some critics have, that dispositional analysis, when applied to 'mental conduct concepts', is a kind of *behaviourism*. For the distinction between dispositions and occurrences cuts across that between what is covert and what is overt, so that some exercises of most human dispositional characteristics will be overt, while others will be covert. My complaint is rather that, as an account of what have often been called 'teleological explanations', dispositional analysis is a kind of *spectatorism*. It misconstrues the logic of typical explanations of human actions because it manœuvres the investigator into considering them from the wrong standpoint. There is a sense of 'explain' in which an action is only explained when it is seen in a context of rational deliberation; when it is seen from the point of view of an agent. Ryle appears to me to be a much safer guide to the analysis of such explanations when, at several points in *The Concept of Mind*, he represents understanding another person's action as a matter of 'following the workings' of his mind.[1] For into this notion could be read most of what I have tried to say about rational explanation.

7. *Dispositions, Reasons, and Causes*

There is one other question arising out of Gardiner's dispositional theory which requires comment if we are not to be misled about the nature of explanation of action in history. Gardiner, like Ryle, draws a sharp distinction between dispositional and causal explanation; he says, for instance, that the statement, 'John hit you with a hammer because he is bad-tempered' cannot be "reduced to an explanation asserting a causal relation between two events or processes, one of which is labelled 'John's bad temper' ". But although this is true, Gardiner appears to me to reach his conclusion for the wrong reason, i.e. that motives like 'bad temper' since they are to be

[1] p. 61.

analysed as dispositions to behave in certain ways, rather than as occurrences, cannot be causes. At one point, for instance, he says that motive explanations are "not causal at all".[1] In this he appears to follow Ryle, who, in *The Concept of Mind*, declared: "Motives are not happenings, and are therefore not of the right type to be causes."[2]

That this conclusion cannot be correct is strongly suggested by the very common citation of dispositional characteristics as causes by historians. Sir David Keir, having pointed out that, following English reverses in the Dutch War of 1665-7, there was "a new encroachment on the Prerogative" by the Commons, observes: "Charles' resentment at this intrusion was undoubtedly one of the many causes which led him to abandon Clarendon to impeachment in 1667."[3] And some of the dispositional examples noted in the preceding section could easily be recast into causal form—for instance, 'The cause of the fatal policy of Charles I was his love of order and ignorance of mankind', or 'It was Disraeli's ambition which caused his attack on Peel in 1646'. What modifications should be made in the Ryle–Gardiner theory in the light of such cases?

I do not think that the admission that 'bad temper' or 'ambition' or 'ignorance' can be a cause need give any comfort to those who (as Ryle might put it) wish to reinstate the ghost in the machine. For there is no need to assume that because motives, intentions, habits, beliefs, and the rest can be causes, they are therefore to be regarded as mental events or processes after all. The error is to be located rather in thinking that only events or processes can be causes, whereas there would seem to be virtually no restriction whatever upon the *type* of thing that can qualify as a cause, provided it passes, in a particular context, what, in Chapter IV, I called the pragmatic and inductive tests. If John would not have hit me had he been good tempered (i.e. the presumption is that the occasion

---

[1] Op. cit., p. 134. Gardiner does deny that explanations are always in terms of events; but this is only to leave room for explanations in terms of (non-causal) dispositions, rather than for causes which are not events (see p. 1).

[2] p. 113.

[3] *Constitutional History of Modern Britain* (4th edn.), 1950, p. 249.

scarcely justified the blow), then his bad temper may be regarded as a necessary condition; and since we may feel that it is high time he took his temper in hand, we may select this necessary condition as the pragmatically important one, and thus call it the cause. As Professor Urmson has pointed out, "what is referred to in one context as a motive may be referred to in another as a cause".[1] It is the context of inquiry which determines whether a dispositional characteristic will be a causal candidate or not.

The apparent logical cleavage between causal and dispositional explanation has sometimes been closed in another way. Mr. P. Alexander, for instance, reminds us that for a disposition to be actualized there must be an occasion—which he calls the cause.[2] A piece of glass shatters when a stone hits it *both* because it has the dispositional property of being brittle and because someone provides a cause by throwing a brick at it. But although I agree that to cite a dispositional property might properly be regarded as an incomplete explanation of what happened if the occasion is unknown, to regard the occasion, rather than the dispositional property, as 'the cause' is to make the mistake already mentioned. It is to assume that causal conditions must be events or processes (while shrinking from admitting that they may be 'mental' ones). Alexander thinks that to call a motive a cause "would be absurd". But this supposed absurdity is actually a commonplace. A dispositional characteristic is a type of 'standing condition'; and standing conditions, as well as precipitating ones, can be causes.

The distinction between causal and dispositional explanation, although it is important to draw it, should therefore not be drawn in such a way that dispositions *as such* are denied causal status. A somewhat similar qualification will be found necessary if we attempt to draw a logical line between causal and rational explanation, as many philosophers who recognize

---

[1] 'Motives and Causes', *Proceedings of the Aristotelian Society, Supp. Vol.*, 1952, p. 193.
[2] 'Cause and Cure in Psychotherapy', ibid., 1955, p. 34.

a difference between answers in terms of reasons and causes do. For (to put it a little crudely) reasons, too, can be causes.

Consider, for instance, Halévy's explanation of a strike at Newcastle in May 1816: it was, he writes "caused by insufficient wages and the high price of bread".[1] It is surely not misreading what is asserted to say that the conditions here described as the cause are precisely those which were 'taken into account' by the strikers in reaching the decision to stop work. The rational basis of the asserted causal connexion is even more explicitly brought out in the following explanation by D. Thomson of the cleavage between the landed and industrial groups in England in the nineteenth century. He writes:

The use to which the landed interests put their predominance in Parliament to protect themselves in this way at the expense of the industrial populations of the towns and the manufacturing interests caused the first big open split between landed and manufacturing interests. All alike wanted steady and level prices: but the industrial interests, employers and workers alike, wanted this to be at a low level, so as to make wages go further, keep wage-bills low and therefore the cost of manufactured goods low, and enable them to reap maximum benefits in world markets. The cotton-merchants likewise wanted the plentiful import of cheap corn to enable the corn-exporting countries to pay for the manufactured cotton goods that England exported. The landowners and farmers wanted corn-prices stabilized at a high level. Thus two distinct groups of economic interests grew up, bitterly hostile to one another: and this led to the long agitation for the repeal of the Corn Laws, the Free Trade movement as a whole, and the demand for the lessening of the power enjoyed by the agricultural and landed interests in Parliament.[2]

In *Other Minds*, Professor John Wisdom observes, truly, that some causes are very nearly reasons.[3] But this does not quite say what such examples require us to say about the relation between causal and rational explanation; for even this remark preserves the dichotomy. What is required is a qualified restatement of Collingwood's doctrine that in history

[1] Op. cit., vol. ii, p. 10.
[2] *England in the Nineteenth Century*, Harmondsworth, 1950, p. 37.
[3] Oxford, 1952, p. 2.

the term 'cause' is often (he, as we saw in Chapter IV, said 'always') used in Sense I: the sense in which to cause someone to do something is to provide him with a motive for doing it (where 'motive' means 'reason'). As Collingwood himself observed, to be caused to act in this sense does not imply that the agent did not make up his mind to do what he did on the basis of certain rational considerations.[1] It is true that in many cases, we should not say that the agent acted freely; for often providing someone with reasons for doing something, for example, holding a pistol to his head, is precisely what we mean by compelling him to do what he does. But even in such a case, the causal connexion between the pointed pistol and the agent's subsequent behaviour is to be understood in rational terms.

The important point for our account of explanation in history is that the necessity of a causal connexion, when it is actions we are talking about, is very often *rational* necessity. In Chapter IV, in discussing the logic of 'cause', I said that although there are various ways of arguing for a causal assertion, the cause had to be a necessary condition of its effect. But there is more than one kind of necessity; and in history the relevant kind will often be that found in action done for a good reason (from the agent's point of view). In the situation sketched by Halévy, for instance, if we are to establish the causal connexion between the strike and the "insufficient wages and the high price of bread", we shall have to fill out the circumstances, beliefs, &c., of the strikers to the point where we can say that without the additional conditions cited, there would have been insufficient reason for going out.

Is there no important difference, then, between saying of the action of a rational agent, 'A's reason for doing x was y', and saying 'The cause of A's doing x was y'? The difference, I think, is one of approach, or point of view, or kind of inquiry. To say the first sort of thing is—as has been suggested at length in the present chapter—to adopt the point of view of an agent. To say the second is to adopt the point of view of a

[1] *An Essay on Metaphysics*, p. 290.

manipulator—although of one well aware that he is dealing with agents who act on rational considerations. Butterfield, in the passage quoted in section 1, contrasts empathetic understanding with "a causal or stand-offish attitude"; and this distinction remains even when it is admitted that the cause of an action may be that which provides the agent with a reason for doing what was done. And it is a fact of ordinary historical writing that historians do sometimes take up this 'stand-offish' attitude in explaining even the rational behaviour of their characters.

VI

EXPLAINING WHY AND EXPLAINING HOW

1. *Explanation Without 'Why' Questions*

IN the preceding chapters my argument against the covering law model has avoided challenging a very common assumption about the logic of 'explanation': the assumption that explanation is given, or when fully stated would be given, in the form of a 'because' answer to a 'why' question. Mr. J. Cohen, for instance, makes it one of three general requirements of explanation that it be an "appropriate answer to the question 'why' the explicandum is the case".[1] Similarly, when Professor Braithwaite attempts to characterize explanation in general, he says it is simply "any answer to a 'why' question which in any way answers the question, and thereby gives some degree of intellectual satisfaction to the questioner . . .";[2] and Professor Ryle, as we noted in Chapter III, discusses explanation as if it were invariably expressed in statements of the form, '. . . because . . .'. Even when no such explicit declarations are made, discussions of explanation are usually confined to an examination of answers to the question 'Why?' And even when we *are* warned that there are other kinds of explanation, the philosophers who warn us seldom go on to say what the peculiarities of the other kinds are.[3]

Since a large proportion of explanations are in fact given in answer to 'why' questions, this special emphasis may be regarded as a very natural and proper one. But if we are to assess the adequacy of the covering law model as a general

[1] 'Teleological Explanation', p. 256. Cohen admits that he here *stipulates* a sense for 'explanation' rather than describes the way the term has in fact been used. But his sketch of what such a sense leaves out does not include answers to other questions than 'Why?'.

[2] 'Teleological Explanation', *Proceedings of the Aristotelian Society*, 1946–7, p. ii.

[3] See, for instance, J. Hospers, 'On Explanation', *Journal of Philosophy*, 1946, p. 337.

theory of explanation in history, it is important to notice that explanations which cannot plausibly be regarded as answers to 'why' questions do quite frequently occur in historical narrative. For I think it can be shown that at least some of them raise difficulties for covering law theory. In the limited space still at my disposal, I cannot attempt to discuss at all fully the way in which the logical structure of explanation varies with the question asked. The fact that I draw attention to only one additional type of explanation to illustrate this thesis here should not, however, be taken to imply that I think there are no further types to be examined.[1]

I shall argue in this chapter that there is an important distinction to be drawn between explaining why a thing happened and answering a certain kind of 'how' question about it. In the latter case, I shall maintain, the historian need not show that what is to be explained happened *necessarily* in the light of the particular events and conditions mentioned in the explanation, and, *a fortiori*, need not show that it happened necessarily in the light of some covering law or laws. For the demand for explanation is, in some contexts, satisfactorily met if what happened is merely shown to have been *possible*; there is no need to go on to show that it was necessary as well. To put the point another way, I shall argue that although, as Professor Toulmin puts it, to explain a thing is often to "show that it might have been expected",[2] the appropriate criterion for one important range of cases is broader than this; for to explain a thing is sometimes merely to show that it need not have caused surprise.

In earlier chapters I have argued that, in typical historical contexts, subsumption of case under covering law is not a necessary condition of giving a satisfactory answer to the question 'Why?' itself. In Chapter II, for instance, I denied that prior knowledge of a covering empirical law was a necessary condition of explaining a unique event on the ground

---

[1] Explanations are often, for instance, answers to 'what' questions; they explain what really happened.

[2] *The Place of Reason in Ethics*, Cambridge, 1950, p. 96.

that the historian could judge in a particular case that there
was a necessary connexion between the event and the circumstances cited to explain it. In Chapter IV, I pointed out that
a causal 'Why?' generally required the isolation of some insufficient condition of the event to be explained, and that it
was quite unnecessary, in doing this, to show that a causal
routine was instantiated. In Chapter V, I argued that when a
human action is explained by reference to the principle which
it applies, the force of the explanation does not depend upon
the truth of the assertion that all men, or even any sub-class
of them, apply such a principle in such circumstances. But
the considerations I now wish to urge against the covering law
theory in respect of explanations in answer to 'how' questions,
are quite independent of all these. For the way in which the
explanations now to be examined depart from the covering
law model is different from that of any type of explanation
examined so far.

In the first of the two sections following, I shall try to make
clear the logical structure of the kind of explanation which I
have in mind, going on thereafter to show the extent to which
some historical explanations display the same structure. In
the second section I shall consider briefly certain likely misunderstandings of, and objections to, the logical point argued for.

2. Explaining How Something Could Be So

The following extract from the 'Parade' column of a popular
magazine provides a simple, sharply defined example of a sort of
explanation which is often given in the ordinary course of affairs :

An announcer broadcasting a baseball game from Victoria, B.C., said:
"It's a long fly ball to centre field, and it's going to hit high up on the
fence. The centre fielder's back, he's under it, he's caught it, and the
batter is out." Listeners who knew the fence was twenty feet high
couldn't figure out how the fielder caught the ball. Spectators could
have given them the unlikely explanation. At the rear of centre field was
a high platform for the scorekeeper. The centre fielder ran up the ladder
and caught the ball twenty feet above the ground.[1]

[1] *Maclean's Magazine*, 1 Aug. 1952 (back cover). I discussed this example
in a similar way in 'Explanatory Narrative in History', *The Philosophical
Quarterly*, 1954, pp. 15–27.

Now in what does such an explanation consist? By comparison with examples considered in previous chapters, it is peculiar in important respects. What is explained—the catch —is the action of a rational agent, yet an explanation in terms of his reasons for doing what he did is not what is required. It would be easy enough to think of occasions on which a rational explanation of such a catch might be demanded and given. If the fielder had been 'dragging his feet' all season, we might very well ask, in surprise: 'Why this efficient display by Braun?'; and in such circumstances the threat of a salary cut might significantly be mentioned. But this is the wrong sort of answer to give to the demand for explanation which arises out of the circumstances supposed here.

To cite a covering empirical generalization, however, would be just as inappropriate. Doubtless the knowledgeable radio audience is well aware that in baseball—at any rate in organized league play—fielders usually catch long fly balls. But although there is usually nothing to wonder at when catches are made by centre-fielders, there is a real mystery about this particular case. What puzzles us is how the fielder managed to get his hand on the ball in view of the fact that the fence was 20 feet high. No generalizations about fielders catching long fly balls, even if known, are of interest in the present case until this prior problem has been solved. And once we learn about the scorekeeper's platform, it would be superfluous to call such generalizations to mind.

The point is not that baseball provides us with an intuitively intelligible subject-matter, so that what happens on the ball field is understandable without our knowing what causes it to happen, or what general laws it instantiates, or what reasons there are for doing what was done. The point is rather that to go on to mention such things would be appropriate only in the face of a *further* demand for explanation—and for explanation of a different kind. In the example we are considering, it is reasonable to assume from the context that there would be no such further demand. The problem which generates the demand for explanation here is not 'What made that happen?', or 'What was his motive for doing that?', but rather 'How could that have happened, in the light of so-and-so?' Explanation is called for because what happened seemed *impossible* under the circumstances.

What *were* the circumstances? It may seem perhaps that these have been disingenuously misrepresented as I have presented the problem. For the question seems at first to be: 'How could the fielder have caught the ball at the twenty-foot mark, with absolutely nothing to stand on?', whereas in fact, there was a perfectly solid platform available, with a ladder attached. We assumed that we were dealing with a case of a fielder catching the ball 20 feet in the air, whereas it was really a case of his catching it from a 20-foot platform. All that the so-called explanation seems to have done is correct our first erroneous impression of what the *facts* of the situation really were. And this, as far as it goes, is perfectly correct.

But if we leave it at that we may be tempted to say one or other of two equally unsatisfactory things: either that nothing happened which required explaining, or that what is offered as explanation is just part of an ordinary answer to a 'why' question. For it might be said, on the one hand, that once the secret is out—once we get the facts straight—we must acknowledge that the original demand for explanation was just a mistake. The spectators in the stands were not mystified by the catch; the radio audience was just a little behind them in learning what actually took place. Being told that there was a ladder and that the fielder ran up it, merely lets us know how in fact the ball was caught. Yet such filling in of missing information would surely, in the circumstances envisaged, be called explanatory. We might imagine a member of the now enlightened radio audience trying the puzzle on a friend, going on after a suitable interval to give him 'the explanation'. But if we go on then to insist that if we do call this revision of our factual knowledge explanatory, it must be because we covertly recognize the fact that it clears the way for ordinary causal or rational explanation to be given, we shall still be in difficulties. For it would surely be quite possible to say, on hearing about

the platform and how the fielder used it, that the catch was
now explained, although we had not the slightest idea what the
centre-fielder's motives were, or whether catches off the platform were regular occurrences. The explanation appears to be
complete without raising such questions at all.

If we are to bring out the force of such explanation, it is not
enough merely to say that it involves correcting our conception
of the facts of the situation. We must ask, 'Why these facts
rather than some other ones?' The particular facts cited in this
case are explanatory because they successfully rebut a presumption—reasonable enough in the light of our knowledge of
the moment—that the fielder could not have caught the ball.
The presumption is that, in spite of the announcement that
the ball was caught, this just *couldn't* have happened; and because of this we are very much surprised when told that it was.
We feel like protesting: 'Fielders can't jump twenty feet into
the air'—and yet we are not prepared actually to *disbelieve* the
announcer's claim that the ball was caught. An explanation is
called for because we cannot reconcile what we know, or think
we know, with an alleged fact which we are nevertheless inclined to accept on independent grounds (e.g. the reputation
of the announcer for accurate sports reporting). What we know
seems to rule out the possibility of the occurrence which is to be
explained. The explanation consists in showing that in spite of
appearances to the contrary, it is not an impossible one after all.

The logical structure of such explanations may appear more
clearly if we compare it with the structure of explanatory
answers to the question 'Why?' In explaining why something
happened, if a presumption enters at all, we rebut a presumption that it *need not* have happened, by showing that, in the
light of certain considerations (perhaps laws as well as facts), it
had to happen. But in explaining how something could have
happened, we rebut the presumption that it *could not* have
happened, by showing that, in the light of certain further facts,
there is after all no good reason for supposing that it could not
have happened. Let us call these explaining *why-necessarily*
and explaining *how-possibly* respectively. The two kinds, in

spite of the parallel drawn between them, are logically independent in the sense that they have different tasks to perform. They are answers to different kinds of questions.

Explanations of the how-possibly pattern are often to be found in ordinary historical writing. The historian's problem is often to explain how some later event or condition could have come to pass in spite of known earlier conditions which give rise to a contrary expectation. If an historian sets out, for instance, to study the Hanoverian succession and settlement, what might he feel obliged to explain? Perhaps, very roughly, the fact that the initiative and power of the British Crown was, for the moment at least, less than that of Parliament. Many kinds of explanation of this fact might be sought and given. Various causes and standing conditions could be cited—the personal qualities of the new king, which made it unlikely that Parliament's position would be challenged; the general temper of the politically articulate classes; the growing economic power of the men who sat in the House of Commons, and so on. Constitutional historians, interested in the way institutions work, might seek to give a functional explanation, in terms of the roles of King and Parliament in the new machinery of government, showing that each had a part to play. In 'scientific' histories we might even be referred to certain general laws of political development. But the historian is just as likely to put his problem in some such form as: 'How could this constitutional situation have come about?'

The historian will say, in effect:

It is certainly strange at first sight to find the Crown taking second place in the constitutional arrangements of 1714 when you remember how Elizabeth used to bend her parliaments to her purposes. A student of the constitutional affairs of the late sixteenth century would have been very much surprised at things turning out this way. If we are to understand how such great changes could have come about in the intervening years, we shall have to look closely at the actual course of events. It is only by filling in these missing details that the disparity can be resolved.

The historian must discover the 'ladder' which, when known, removes the appearance of discrepancy between the consti-

tutional positions of the Crown under Tudors and Hano-
verians.

The 'ladder' in historical cases need not, of course, be as
complicated as this. It is suggested, for instance, by M. Ashley,
in his *England in the 17th Century*, that the explanation of the
dissolution of the Short Parliament in 1640 is to be found in
the late arrival of Laud and Strafford at the Privy Council
meeting at which the decision was taken.[1] The force of such
explanation is not to show *why* this unlikely decision was
taken; it is to show *how it was that it was taken* in spite of the
presumption that it would not be—a presumption arising out of
Ashley's presentation of Strafford as a man of great influence,
and as opposed to the dissolution. The explanation rebuts the
presumption that Strafford would have prevented what actually happened, by recording the hard fact that he simply
wasn't there.

In still other cases, a logical pattern can be discovered
which is, at any rate, similar to the one just noted, for example,
in the following explanation by Trevelyan of the success of
the Revolution of 1688–9:

In the affair of the Revolution the element of chance, of sheer good
luck, was dominant. It was only the accident of James II that gave our
ancestors the opportunity to right themselves. At the end of Charles II's
reign nothing seemed less probable than that England would soon
become either a powerful state or a free and peaceful land. The violence
of her factions for half a century past had reduced her to prostration
before a royal despotism in the pay of France. One of two things
seemed certain: either the system would continue unchallenged till all
religious and political Dissent had been crushed out of existence and
till France had conquered Western Europe; or else another turn of the
tables, possibly another civil war, would produce another violent over-
turn, but no true 'settlement'. Nothing could really have saved England
except the apparently impossible—a reconciliation of Tory and Whig,
Church and Dissent. That miracle was wrought by the advent of James
II, who united against himself the old antagonists. The eleventh-hour
chance thus given to our ancestors was neither missed nor abused.[2]

In this example, it is true, the presumption which is rebutted

---

[1] Harmondsworth, 1952, p. 72.
[2] *The English Revolution*, pp. 240–1.

is cautiously represented as a mere 'probability'. But the demand for explanation clearly arises out of the apparent unlikelihood of what happened in the light of what was known about the preceding situation. And the explanation is given by showing that with the addition of James II to that situation, the presumption of improbability no longer holds good.

3. How-possibly and Why-necessarily

I have tried in the preceding section to mark off a type of explanation often given in answer to a 'how' question, and to show that many explanations in history approximate more closely to this 'how-possibly' model than to the model of the covering law. Let me go on to sharpen my account of the way explaining how something could be so differs from explaining why it is so by considering some likely misconceptions of, and objections to, what I have said so far.

Some misunderstandings of the argument advanced will probably arise out of my saying that explanation can be given by merely showing that what happened was *possible*. It may be thought, for instance, that in arguing for the legitimacy of such 'possibility' explanations, and in claiming that they are important in history, I am surreptitiously taking sides in the traditional dispute between determinists and libertarians. It may appear that a type of explanation which consists merely of showing that a certain course of action was 'open', and which stops short of requiring, say, that an agent's adoption of that course of action was necessitated by his circumstances, his character, his training, and so on, is peculiarly appropriate to a study like history, which deals with the actions of men who possess some degree of freedom of choice. The covering law model, with its requirement that if an action is to be explicable, it must be shown to be predictable, has always seemed unacceptable to some of its opponents because it appears to put free actions beyond the scope of explanation altogether. And the how-possibly model may perhaps be thought to show how such actions can, after all, be accounted for, short of meeting this demand.

I must insist, however, that the logical distinction which has been drawn between explaining something how-possibly and showing it to have been predictable, has not the slightest relevance to the free will question. For the independence of the two questions can be shown not only for human actions, but for what happens to inanimate objects as well. Suppose that a person is told that the resort he is in the habit of visiting each year has been destroyed by an avalanche. 'That's impossible!' he may protest; 'There's never enough snow on those hills to guarantee a decent day's skiing'. The sort of explanation required by this objector would include an account of the unprecedentedly severe winter which preceded the disaster. Adding further facts to the stock he was working with would relieve the logical tension between what he already knows and what he is now asked to believe. His perfectly reasonable presumption must be rebutted; he must be shown that there could have been an avalanche after all. The essential feature of explaining how-possibly is thus not that it is given of happenings which cannot be brought under law. It is rather that it is given in the face of a certain sort of puzzlement.

In many cases, both in explaining human actions and explaining natural events, it will be *empirical* knowledge which gives rise to the protest: 'That's impossible!' But it is important for an understanding of historical cases to realize that the notion of 'possibility' must often be taken more broadly than that. For there are many kinds of possibility: physical, logical, rational, moral, &c. (just as there are kinds of necessity). If an historical agent fails to do something which his purposes and principles would seem to require him to do, a how-possibly explanation may take the form of showing that his principles were in fact otherwise, or that he did not in this case appreciate the nature of his situation. In this way a presumption of impossibility in the rational sense would be rebutted. The distinction I wish to draw between explanations in terms of possibility and necessity thus cuts across the distinction drawn in Chapter V between rational and non-rational explanations. And in history, since the context of discussion is an account of human actions, it is to be expected that explaining how-possibly will generally be in terms of rational possibility.

It is important for me to make it clear, too, that in presenting 'how-possibly' explanations as a distinct type, I do not pretend that all explanations employing the notion of 'possibility' will display the presumption-rebuttal pattern which has been elicited here. For in many cases, especially in rational explanation of actions, answers to 'why' questions may also turn on this notion. Their force will often derive from showing that no other course was possible to the agent, under the circumstances, than the one he in fact took; and this, of course, is to represent the action as *necessary* (in the appropriate sense). The following example from Halévy's *History of the English People in the Nineteenth Century*, illustrates the point:

> It was impossible to ask for an extension of the protection given to cereals by the Act of 1815; for that Act prohibited the import of corn at a price below 80s a quarter, and the present price barely exceeded 50s. The utmost they could ask was that the prohibition be made more stringent by repealing the clause which permitted the foreign importer to store his grain in the British warehouse. . . .[1]

Halévy here explains the failure to extend the 1815 Act by showing that this was impossible. This pattern of explanation —the accounting for a non-occurrence by reference to an impossibility—is very common in history. But it is quite different logically from the type we have been discussing here.

It is equally important for me to make it clear that not all answers to 'how' questions are 'how-possibly' explanations. 'Explaining how' may sometimes, for instance, be in terms of a method of doing something, rather than an account of happenings. We ask: 'How do you change a tyre on a Morris Minor?', and get a reply phrased in a timeless idiom. 'Explaining how' may also mean making clear the detailed steps or stages by which something came about. Thus Chester Wilmot states the theme of his recent book, *The Struggle for Europe*, as: "Not only how Hitler was overthrown but how Stalin

[1] Op. cit., vol. ii, p. 5.

emerged victorious, how Russia came to replace Germany as the dominant power in Europe, and how Stalin succeeded in obtaining from Roosevelt and Churchill what he failed to obtain from Hitler."[1] This sense of 'explaining how' is a very common one in history, but it is quite different from explaining how something could be so. Indeed, a covering law theorist might argue with some plausibility that explaining how something came about is different from explaining why it happened only in the fact that in the first case there would be an *essential* inclusion of the details, in a fairly strict temporal sequence, whereas in the second case there is at least a suggestion that certain considerations ought to be picked out—and that an order of importance, rather than of time, would be employed. And it would be difficult to deny that if a complete explanation had been given of how something came about, the explicandum would be rendered at least as predictable as it would have been by a corresponding explanation why. In this respect, explaining how something came about is more like explaining why than like explaining how-possibly.

The chief objection to my distinction between explaining how-possibly and explaining why-necessarily will no doubt be that, although there are interesting differences between them, they do not justify my claiming that the two kinds of explanation are logically independent. It may be argued that although, in answer to a 'how-possibly' question, all that need be mentioned is the presence of some previously unsuspected necessary condition of what happened—the fielder's ladder, or Strafford's absence, or the stupidity of James II—nevertheless this does not amount to a full explanation of what happened. In so far as the explanation stops short of indicating sufficient conditions, and, at any rate implicitly, appealing to a covering law, it will be said to be defective—an incomplete explanation, which can only be completed by transforming it into an appropriate answer to a corresponding 'Why?'

Now there is at least this much excuse for regarding a why-necessarily explanation as more 'fundamental' than a

[1] London, 1952, preface

how-possibly: that, having given a how-possibly answer, it always makes sense to go on to demand a why-necessarily one, whereas this relationship does not hold in the opposite direction. Having been told why something happened, to go on to ask 'How?' could only mean 'how it came about', not 'how it could be so'—it would be to ask for more details to be filled in. But this is not to say that a how-possibly answer cannot be quite complete *with respect to its own peculiar kind of question*, without enlarging it to a specification of the conditions from which the explained event could have been predicted—perhaps in accordance with a covering law.

To insist, nevertheless, that no explanation is complete until a lurking covering law has been discovered is surely just to fall into a kind of determinist myopia. Such a claim finds little warrant, at any rate, in an examination of the sort of problem which gives rise to an explanation of how something could be so. It is, of course, always open to a covering law theorist to maintain that the event explained *is* law-covered. But it matters very little for our present discussion whether his claim is based on empirical data in individual cases, or whether it derives from an *a priori* theory that every move we make must instantiate a law. For claiming that a certain happening *is* law-covered is quite different from claiming that the alleged covering law is *required* in order to give an explanation; and reasons have already been given for thinking that it would *not* be required in order to resolve the particular kind of puzzlement which is expressed by the question: 'How could that have happened, in the light of so-and-so?' To put the point another way: it is surely not necessary, in order to rebut the presumption that law *A* applies, to show that, in fact, the event in question is governed by a quite different law, law *B*. Let us not try to base a theory of explanation upon the practice of those who insist on answering unasked questions.

If it is objected that, in practice, a 'serious investigator' would soon transform the original 'how' question into a full-blown 'why', we must ask whether this is intended as a statement of fact, or as a point of logic. For I should agree that, in many cases, historians may begin with how-possibly questions and then, after detailed investigation, offer an answer to a 'why' question. But I cannot see that this justifies the claim that an answer stopping short of this in the way outlined is not a logically complete explanation *of its type*. A how-possibly explanation can be complete, without specifying a set of sufficient conditions, in a sense of 'complete' in which an ordinary answer to the question 'Why did this happen?' may not be. For, as we saw in Chapter II, an answer to a 'why' question which gives only some or a few necessary conditions of what is explained, if it is challenged, may have to be added to in order to provide a more satisfactory answer to the *same* question. But in the case of a how-possibly explanation, to demand a set of sufficient conditions would be to *change* the question. Thus, if it were maintained that a 'serious investigator' would have to, or would ultimately have to, supplement with other necessary conditions the kind of answer that merely rebuts a presumption of impossibility, then I must suspect that this investigator is really just the covering law logician in disguise.

NOTES

NOTE A, p. 31. It is interesting to notice that when Hempel offers an example of the way a 'probability hypothesis' may 'cover' an explanation, his theory leads him to analyse the logical structure of the explanation in a very unplausible and artificial way. He points out, for instance: "If Tommy comes down with the measles two weeks after his brother, and if he has not been in the company of other persons having the measles, we accept the explanation that he caught the disease from his brother." According to Hempel, "there is a general hypothesis underlying this explanation; but it can hardly be said to be a general law to the effect that any person who has not had the measles before will get them without fail if he stays in the company of somebody else who has the measles; that a contagion will occur can be asserted only with a high probability". In such cases, and in many historical cases, he claims, the explanation "if fully and explicitly formulated . . . would state certain initial conditions and certain probability hypotheses . . .".

But the case is surely one in which, although we should probably appeal to general medical theory in defending the explanation, our 'law' would be of the form: 'The only way to catch the measles is from someone who has it already.' That Tommy caught the disease from his brother can in fact be *deduced* in this case from the law stated and the statement Hempel gives of the initial condition—"he has not been in the company of other persons having the disease". If we asserted the explanation as a mere probability, this would not be because we used a general 'probability hypothesis', but because we were not entirely sure of the initial condition. What we can be quite sure of, however, is that the mere probability of the general 'hypothesis', 'Whoever exposes himself to someone who has the measles will catch them himself', is quite irrelevant for an assessment of the explanation actually given.

NOTE B, p. 96. There are at least two quite different kinds of situation in which *ceteris paribus* has a clear and unobjectionable employment. There is, first, the kind exemplified above where, having formulated a causal law for a type of situation in which we have found it safe to ignore all but one or a small number of antecedent conditions, the law can be regarded as stating a sufficient condition, *ceteris paribus*. Here the qualifying phrase registers our assumption of a normal application situation for the law.

There is also a familiar use of the expression in contexts where we have explicitly in mind certain limits to the applicability of the law qualified. Such a use is common in theoretical discussions in economics, where, for the purpose of more easily grasping the interrelation of a complicated set of conditions, attention is directed to a few of them at a time. The effects of varying such factors separately is shown by means of 'laws' to which *ceteris paribus* is added to indicate our awareness that in a real situation the relationship envisaged would hardly ever be uncomplicated by the other factors; and the 'law' is thus not to be taken as a guide to prediction and action as it stands.

The use of the expression by some covering law theorists (cf. Gardiner, op. cit., pp. 11–12, 93–94) as a logical bridge by means of which to pass plausibly from a particular explanatory statement to a covering law is different from either of the foregoing. For the 'law' thus obtained does not indicate an abstract relationship which is seldom, if ever, instantiated. Nor does the qualification indicate that in certain standard contexts the 'law' has been found reliable. It merely generalizes a concrete causal relationship found on a particular occasion.

Note C, p. 126. A certain apparent difficulty about our use of the words 'understand' and 'explain' disappears in the light of such a 'scale' of rational explanation. Ordinarily, I think, we tend to assume that these two notions are correlative: when I know the explanation of something then I understand it; and when I understand it, I am in a position to give the explanation. But the relation between the two is more complicated than that, for in many cases we should hesitate to claim understanding of what was done even though we know the explanation. This would probably not often be so in cases where, in order to give a rational explanation, all we have to do is supply the agent's beliefs, whether correct or not. But if reference has to be made to quite peculiar purposes and principles in the calculation we shall probably be less comfortable—and show it by hedging a little about the propriety of saying we 'understand' the action thus explained. In a sense we understand a certain action so long as, not our principles, but the agent's, enjoin it. But if we find his principles uncommonly wrong-headed, or perhaps in moral cases even revolting, we may want to say: 'Although I see how he figured it out, I find it quite impossible to understand his acting that way.' That is, we allow our notions of 'explanation' and 'understanding' to get out of step in order to register our awareness of just how far we are having to descend the scale in order to achieve what I have called an explanatory equilibrium.

Note D, p. 132. It may be of interest, in this connexion, to refer back to Gardiner's parallel from the practical sphere: the case of the general who is forced to make up his mind what course of action to take. For it might be claimed that this case is even more appropriate for elucidating the logic of the explanation of action in history than Gardiner seems to have realized. In Chapter II, I argued that the general's decision was like typical explanations of historical events in that it required *judgement*, it did not apply pre-formulated general knowledge 'covering' the particular case. But the general's decision is also like typical explanations of individual actions in history in that, if a tremendously complicated general statement *were* extracted from the decision reached, it would be a principle of action rather than a generalization.

Note E, p. 146. This point appears to be misunderstood by Mr. J. Cohen when he argues (in 'Teleological Explanation', *Proceedings of the Aristotelian Society*, 1950–1, p. 268 n.) that "it is always possible to unpack a law from a dispositional explanans". Cohen points out that, although from the explanation, "She slammed the door because she was angry", we cannot assume the truth of the 'law', "She always slams doors when angry", this really only requires us to say that "the explanatory law requires qualification" to a greater extent when derived from a dispositional statement. (This would be due to what Ryle called the highly determinable character of the dispositional term.)

But Cohen's 'law' is a law of a particular thing, rather than of a type or kind of thing. It would not, I think, be counted a law at all by covering law theorists.

INDEX OF NAMES

PRINTED IN GREAT BRITAIN
AT THE UNIVERSITY PRESS, OXFORD
BY VIVIAN RIDLER
PRINTER TO THE UNIVERSITY